Workshop on Processing Language Variation: Digital Armenian (DigitAm 2022)

Held at LREC 2022

Marseille, France
20 – 25 June 2022

Editors:

Victoria Khurshudyan
Nadi Tomeh
Damien Nouvel
Anaid Donabedian
Chahan Vidal-Gorene

ISBN: 978-1-7138-6118-8

Printed from e-media with permission by:

Curran Associates, Inc.
57 Morehouse Lane
Red Hook, NY 12571

CURRAN ASSOCIATES INC.
proceedings.com

Some format issues inherent in the e-media version may also appear in this print version.

Association for Computational Linguistics
209 N. Eighth Street
Stroudsburg, Pennsylvania 18360

Phone: 1-570-476-8006
Fax: 1-570-476-0860

acl@aclweb.org

Additional copies of this publication are available from:

Curran Associates, Inc.
57 Morehouse Lane
Red Hook, NY 12571 USA
Phone: 845-758-0400
Fax: 845-758-2633
Email: curran@proceedings.com
Web: www.proceedings.com

LREC 2022 Workshop
Language Resources and Evaluation Conference
20-25 June 2022

Workshop on Processing Language Variation: Digital Armenian (DigitAm)

Editors:
Victoria Khurshudyan, Nadi Tomeh, Damien Nouvel, Anaid Donabedian, Chahan Vidal-Gorene

Proceedings of the LREC 2022 workshop on Processing Language Variation: Digital Armenian (DigitAm)

Edited by:
Victoria Khurshudyan, Nadi Tomeh, Damien Nouvel, Anaid Donabedian, Chahan Vidal-Gorene

For more information:
European Language Resources Association (ELRA)
9 rue des Cordelires
75013, Paris
France
http://www.elra.info
Email: lrec@elda.org

Preface

This volume includes the proceedings of the workshop Processing Language Variation: Digital Armenian held in Marseille, France, June 20, 2022. It is organized by the team of DALiH project: Digitizing Armenian Linguistic Heritage (DALiH)[1]: Armenian Multi-variational Corpus and Data Processing, more particularly by the three research centres: Structure et Dynamique des Langues (SeDyL)/INALCO, Laboratoire d'Informatique de Paris-Nord (LIPN) /Université Sorbonne Paris Nord and Équipe de Recherche Textes, Informatique, Multilinguisme (ERTIM)/INALCO. The workshop is in line with the international conference Digital Armenian first held in Paris, INALCO, in 2019.

The workshop welcomed papers on exploring the problems connected with language variation processing through interoperability of NLP and linguistic resources and tools in particular (but not limited to) for multi-variational under-resourced languages, multi-variational corpora designing and functionality, the evaluation of language scalar variation and the degree of interoperability relevance, language variety identification and distance measuring etc.

A significant gap exists for the availability of NLP resources for different languages with a few languages having quasi-complete NLP coverage and many others being under-resourced (or no-resourced at all). Besides, the under-resourced languages can often have variation either at synchronic (dialects, oral vernacular varieties) or diachronic level (ancient variants of a target language) for which resources can be completely absent especially if no written tradition exists for a target variety. The workshop will focus on processing and reutilisation of NLP resources for under-resourced languages with variation in general, with a particular attention to the Armenian language data.

Current state-of-the-art NLP approaches open up remarkable perspectives not only to exploit the available NLP resources of the well-resourced languages for the under-resourced ones, but also to recycle the existing resources of a target language for its varieties (multi-variational resources) instead of processing target language/variety-based new NLP resources from scratch.

The existing resources are often heterogeneous in terms of accessibility, formatting, linguistic background and they are usually specialized in only one type of a tool/resource (scanned text and/or plain-text databases, dictionaries, annotation models/tools, annotated corpora and datasets etc.). Therefore, one of the important issues is to work out approaches and standards of harmonization and interoperability of the existing data and resources.

Overall, six papers were selected for the workshop. Two papers focus on different aspects of Classical and Middle Armenian linguistic data processing (Analyse Automatique de l'Ancien Arménien. Évaluation d'une méthode hybride « dictionnaire » et « réseau de neurones » sur un Extrait de l'Adversus Haereses d'Irénée de Lyon by Kepeklian and Kindt; and Describing Language Variation in the Colophons of Armenian Manuscripts by Van Elverdinghe and Kindt) and one paper explores the variational identification for Classical Armenian and two modern standards (Dialects Identification of Armenian Language by Avetisyan). Modern Armenian standards are targeted in the paper presenting a morphological transducer for Modern Western Armenian (A Free/Open-Source Morphological Transducer for Western Armenian by Dolatian et al.), and another on Eastern Armenian National Corpus (Eastern Armenian National Corpus: State of the Art and Perspectives by Khurshudyan et al.), Finally, one paper explores the possibilities of Automatic Speech Recognition model (ASR) model processing for modern Armenian varieties (Towards a Unified ASR System for the Armenian Standards by Chakmakjian and Wang).

Workshop Organizers

[1]The project DALiH is funded by French National Research Agency ANR-21-CE38-0006.

Organizers

Victoria Khurshudyan – Inalco, Sedyl, CNRS
Anaid Donabedian – Inalco, Sedyl, CNRS
Chahan Vidal-Gorene – École Nationale des Chartes-PSL
Nadi Tomeh – LIPN, Université Sorbonne Paris Nord
Damien Nouvel – INALCO, ERTIM

Program Committee:

Victoria Khurshudyan, Inalco, Sedyl, CNRS, IRD
Anaid Donabedian, Inalco, Sedyl, CNRS, IRD
Chahan Vidal-Gorene, École Nationale des Chartes-PSL
Nadi Tomeh, LIPN, Université Sorbonne Paris Nord
Damien Nouvel, Inalco, ERTIM
Emmanuel Cartier, LIPN, Université Sorbonne Paris Nord
Thierry Charnois, LIPN, Université Sorbonne Paris Nord
Ilaine Wang, Inalco, ERTIM
Vladimir Plungian, Vinogradov Russian Language Institute, Russian Academy of Sciences
Timofey Arkhangelskiy, University of Hamburg

Table of Contents

Conference Program

2:00pm–2:20pm Opening with a presentation on the project of Digitizing Armenian Linguistic Heritage (DALiH): Armenian Multivariational Corpus and Data Processing
Victoria Khurshudyan

Session 1

2:20pm–2:40pm	*A Free/Open-Source Morphological Transducer for Western Armenian* Hossep Dolatian, Daniel Swanson and Jonathan Washington
2:40pm–3:00pm	*Dialects Identification of Armenian Language* Karen Avetisyan
3:00pm–3:20pm	*Analyse Automatique de l'Ancien Arménien. Évaluation d'une méthode hybride « dictionnaire » et « réseau de neurones » sur un Extrait de l'Adversus Haereses d'Irénée de Lyon* Bastien Kindt and Gabriel Kepeklian
3:20pm–3:40pm	*Describing Language Variation in the Colophons of Armenian Manuscripts* Bastien Kindt and Emmanuel Van Elverdinghe
3:40pm–4:00pm	*Eastern Armenian National Corpus: State of the Art and Perspectives* Victoria Khurshudyan, Timofey Arkhangelskiy, Misha Daniel, Vladimir Plungian, Dmitri Levonian, Alex Polyakov and Sergei Rubakov

Session 2

4:30pm–4:50pm	*Towards a Unified ASR System for the Armenian Standards* Samuel Chakmakjian and Ilaine Wang
4:50pm–5:50pm	***Round table***

5:50pm–6:00pm Closing remarks
Viktoria Khurshudyan

Proceedings of the Workshop on Processing Language Variation: Digital Armenian (DigitAm 2022) @LREC2022, pages 1–7
Marseille, 20 June 2022

A Free/Open-Source Morphological Transducer for Western Armenian

Hossep Dolatian, Daniel Swanson, Jonathan Washington
Stony Brook University, Indiana University, Swarthmore College
Stony Brook, NY 11794; Bloomington, IN 47405; Swarthmore, PA 19081
hossep.dolatian@alumni.stonybrook.edu, dangswan@iu.edu, jonathan.washington@swarthmore.edu

Abstract

We present a free/open-source morphological transducer for Western Armenian, an endangered and low-resource Indo-European language. The transducer has virtually complete coverage of the language's inflectional morphology. We built the lexicon by scraping online dictionaries. As of submission, the transducer has a lexicon of 75K words. It has over 90% naive coverage on different Western Armenian corpora, and high precision.

Keywords: finite-state morphology, two-level morphology, transducer, computational morphology, low-resource language, Western Armenian

1. Introduction

This paper presents the first known publicly available morphological transducer for Western Armenian (hyw), an endangered Indo-European language currently spoken by an estimated 1 million people (Eberhard et al., 2022).[1] A morphological transducer is a computational tool that maps between forms and analyses, able to perform both morphological analysis and morphological generation. For example, the form բառերեն [pʰɑɾeɾen] 'the words' may be analyzed as բառ<n><pl><abl><def>, whereas generation goes the other direction. The morphological transducer reported on in this paper has production-quality coverage and was developed entirely by hand, with some automated support in the form of scraping dictionaries.

Section 2 overviews Western Armenian and positions the present work among other Armenian text processing tools. Section 3 details the implementation of the transducer. Section 4 presents an evaluation of the transducer. Section 5 presents thoughts on future work, and Section 6 focuses on cross-dialectal support. Section 7 concludes.

2. Background on Armenian and language tools

Armenian belongs to an independent branch in the Indo-European family. Armenian is pluricentric with two standard lects (Western and Eastern) and multiple non-standard lects (Adjarian, 1909). The two standard lects share substantial similarities but have many substantial differences in phonology, morphology and syntax (Cowe, 1992; Donabédian, 2018). Both lects are written in the Armenian script. Western Armenian uses a more conservative spelling system than Eastern Armenian (Sanjian, 1996; Dum-Tragut, 2009).

Eastern Armenian is the official language of Armenia, while Western Armenian developed as a koiné lect among ethnic Armenians in the Ottoman Empire (Sayeed and Vaux, 2017). After the Armenian Genocide (1915–1917), Western Armenian became a largely diasporic language that is spoken across communities in the Middle East, Europe, the Americas, and Australia. Western Armenian is classified as an endangered language by UNESCO. Depending on the country, Western Armenian communities have different degrees of language maintenance, language shift, or endangerment (Jebejian, 2007; Al-Bataineh, 2015; Chahinian and Bakalian, 2016).

In terms of pre-existing resources, Armenian is considered a low-resource language with few computational resources (Megerdoomian, 2009). There are more resources for Eastern Armenian than for Western.[2] For example, Eastern Armenian has the EANC corpus (Khurshudian et al., 2009), a spoken corpus (Skopeteas et al., 2015), corpus-processing tools like UniParser (Arkhangelskiy et al., 2012), a treebank (Yavrumyan et al., 2017; Yavrumyan, 2019), and various Deep Learning tools from the YerevaNN[3] research group (Ghukasyan et al., 2018; Arakelyan et al., 2018). Eastern Armenian is also part of the Universal Morphology schema (Kirov et al., 2018; Chiarcos et al., 2018; McCarthy et al., 2020).

In contrast, there are few if any significant resources for Western Armenian. There is report of a two-level finite-state system (Lonsdale and Danielyan, 2004) but it does not appear to be available. There are some small corpora of Western Armenian (Donabédian and Boyacioglu, 2007; Khachatryan, 2012; Khachatryan, 2013; Silberztein, 2016), and a new UD treebank (Yavrumyan, 2019).[4] Complete verbal paradigms are also available (Boyacioglu and Dolatian, 2020). Thus any contribution to computer processing of Western Armenian currently

[1] The source code for the transducer is available at `https://github.com/apertium/apertium-hyw`, and the transducer may be used online at `https://beta.apertium.org/#analysis?aLang=hyx_hyw`.

[2] There are likewise recent resources for Classical Armenian (Vidal-Gorène and Decours-Perez, 2020; Vidal-Gorène and Kindt, 2020), which have been recently applied to the modern lects (Vidal-Gorène et al., 2020): `https://calfa.fr/`

[3] `http://yerevann.com/`

[4] `https://universaldependencies.org/treebanks/hyw_armtdp/index.html`.

has the potential to make a large impact.

Note that Vidal-Gorène et al. (2020) develop a quite workable model of Eastern and Western Armenian using Deep Learning. However, this paper sees how far we can go with a rule-based system for the following reasons. First, rule-based methods are more interpretable than neural-based methods, so the designer of the analyzer can directly control the behavior of the analyzer. Second, interpretability allows linguists to directly analyze the analyzer to further their own pen-and-paper analyses (Karttunen, 2006); this is quite important for under-studied langauges. Third, rule-based and neural-based methods aren't in true competition with each other because they have different practical uses. Thus, the rule-based analyzer described here can hypothetically integrate with a neural-based analyzer to cover any gaps (cf. finite-state covering grammar in text normalization: Zhang et al. (2019)).

3. Methodology and implementation

3.1. Software

This transducer was written for use with HFST (Lindén et al., 2011) using the two-level framework (Koskenniemi, 1984; Beesley and Karttunen, 2003; Roark and Sproat, 2007).

The lexicon and morphotactics (combinatorial patterns of morphology) were implemented using `lexd` (Swanson and Howell, 2021), which differs from other formalisms in that it is designed to support non-suffixational patterns, like prefixes. The morphophonology (phonological/orthographic alternations) was implemented using `twolc`. The two separate transducers (morphotactic and morphophonological) are compose-intersected to create both a generator and an analyzer. The bulk of the work was done between October 2020 and January 2021.

3.2. Paradigms

In terms of morphology, Western Armenian is largely agglutinative and it is primarily suffixing. There are some inflectional and derivational prefixes. Verb inflection is primarily agglutinative and synthetic with different suffixes for tense, aspect, agreement, mood, and valency. Verbs are divided into different conjugation classes based on suffix allomorphy, root allomorphy, and other irregularities (Boyacioglu, 2010). For these reasons, we chose to use the "infinitive" forms of verbs as the lemmas, instead of the morphological stems. Similarly, noun inflection is primarily agglutinative with different suffixes for number, case, definiteness, and possession (Hagopian, 2005). To illustrate, we present two morphological forms of a verb in (1) and (2), showing orthographic form, IPA pronunciation, a morpheme-by-morpheme breakdown and gloss,[5] an English translation of the form, and the analysis returned by the transducer.

(1) սիրել [siɾel]
sir -e -l
like TH INF
'to like'
սիրել<v><tv><ger>

(2) սիրեցին [siɾet͡sin]
siɾ -e -t͡s -i -n
like TH PFV PST 3PL
'they liked'
սիրել<v><tv><past><pret><p3><pl><indc>

The analyses returned by a transducer differ from traditional linguistic analyses in that morpheme breaks are not provided; tags are used instead of abbreviations; word categories (or parts of speech), here VERB or <v>, are annotated; and subcategories of words, here TRANSITIVE or <tv>, are annotated. This particular transducer also differs in that the infinitive is used as the lemma of a verb instead of the morphological stem, and some grammatical labels are different. The tagset used is that provided by Apertium.[6]

To construct this transducer, morphological paradigms were gathered via a combination of pre-existing teaching grammars of Western Armenian (Boyacioglu, 2010; Hagopian, 2005), using cognates from Eastern Armenian grammars (Dum-Tragut, 2009), and native intuition. All paradigms were manually coded into the `lexd` format.

For an irregular word like ճամբայ [d͡ʒampʰɑ] 'road', the analyzer analyses both standard irregular forms like ճամբու [d͡ʒampʰ-u] (genitive), but also colloquial regularized forms like ճամբայի [d͡ʒampʰɑj-i]. However, the generator only produces the standard form.

We added rules to generate some productive derivational processes as well, such as causativization, passivization, and some productive word-forming suffixes like the suffix -օրէն *-oɾen* (forms adverbs from adjectives, roughly equivalent to the English suffix *-ly*).

For complex verbs like causatives and passives, we adopted a dual approach to lemmatization and analysis. If the dictionary listed a passive verb like ձգուիլ [t͡səkʰ-v-i-l] 'to be left', then that means that this verb likely developed some opaque semantics when compared to the active form ձգել [t͡səkʰ-e-l] 'to let'. We treated such listed passives as their own lemmas. But for most verbs like երգել [jeɾkʰ-e-l] 'to sing', most dictionaries don't list the passive երգուիլ [jeɾkʰə-v-i-l] 'to be sung' because the morphology and semantics are predictable. For such unlisted passives, we derive them at run-time from the lemma of the active. Similar annotation and strategies are used for causatives.

3.3. Lexicon

The lexicon was at first compiled by scraping an Armenian-English dictionary (Kouyoumdjian, 1970) from Nayiri.[7] The dictionary contained at least 60k words.

[5] Glossing conventions and abbreviations are based on Leipzig standards: https://www.eva.mpg.de/lingua/resources/glossing-rules.php

[6] https://wiki.apertium.org/wiki/Symbols

[7] http://nayiri.com/

The dictionary items were catalogued into the right conjugation or declension class. A sample of common Armenian names was gathered from lists of names on different websites.[8] Table 1 provides a breakdown of the lexicon.[9]

	category	entries	tag
Core POS	Noun	39006	<n>
	Adjective	18617	<adj>
	Verb	7441	<v>
	Adverb	1895	<adv>
Names	Given name	4848	<np><ant>
	Surname	2052	<np><cog>
	Location name	1183	<np><top>
	Other name	22	<np><al>
Function, other	Pronoun	415	<prn>
	Adposition	130	<pr>, <post>
	Abbreviation	81	<abbr>
	Conjunction	48	<conj>
	Interjection	49	<ij>
	Numeral	41	<num>
	Particle	9	<particle>
	Total	75837	

Table 1: Current lexicon by part-of-speech

3.4. Morpho-phonology

Some morpho-phonological processes are reflected in the orthography. These were implemented through use of special symbols in the morphological side of the morphotactic transducer (`lexd`). Such symbols encode allomorphy and other morphophonological processes. These diacritics were then used in the morphophonological transducer (`twol`) to trigger the appropriate processes.

As an example, the definite suffix is [ə] after consonants (3a) and [n] after vowels (3b). However, with stems ending in the glide letter յ ‹j› (a consonant), the pattern is slightly different: monosyllabic nouns of this sort (3c) behave as expected: the glide is pronounced and the definite suffix is [ə]. But in multisyllabic stems ending in յ ‹j› (3d), the glide letter is silent when not before a vowel, and is not represented orthographically when before a consonant. Hence, in the definite form, the glide letter is not used, and the suffix [n] is added.

(3) Allomorphy of the definite suffix

a.	բառ	‹paṙ›	[pʰɑɾ]	'word'
	բառը	‹paṙə›	[pʰɑɾ-ə]	'the word'
b.	կատու	‹gadu›	[gɑdu]	'cat'
	կատուն	‹gadun›	[gɑdu-n]	'the cat'
c.	խոյ	‹xoj›	[χoj]	'ram'
	խոյը	‹xojə›	[χoj-ə]	'the ram'
d.	ծառայ	‹d͡zaṙaj›	[d͡zɑɾɑ]	'servant'
	ծառան	‹d͡zaṙan›	[d͡zɑɾɑ-n]	'the servant'

In our code, the definite suffix was generated in the `lexd` file as the symbol `{defՆ}`. The mapping of this to the correct output symbol was conditioned using rules in the `twol` file.

3.5. Infixed punctuation

For punctuation, some punctuation elements are placed outside of words, but others are placed inside words on the stressed vowel. For example, the word [pʰɑ́ɾ] 'word' when unquestioned is spelled բառ ‹paṙ›. When this word is questioned, the interrogative marker is added on top of the stressed letter: բա՞ռ ‹pa$^{?}$ṙ›. Stress is generally predictable in the language as being word-final while ignoring schwas. Some function words have idiosyncratic stress placement. To handle word-internal punctuation, we specified a final punctuation marker for every word in the lexicon (`lexd` file). In another transducer built to handle infixed punctuation, also written in the `lexd` formalism, we defined 'metathesis' rules to move these final punctuation symbols into the correct word-internal location.

For words with irregular stress, the main lexicon file contained a diacritic to mark this irregular stressed location. For example, the word 'how much' has irregular stress on the first vowel: [**vóɾ**kʰɑn]. The question marker is added on the first syllable: ո՞րքան ‹o$^{?}$rk'an›. The lexicon represents this word as ո{՞}րքան with a diacritic question mark. Upon intersection with the punctuation transducer, the value of the question marker is changed, moved, or deleted as needed.

4. Evaluation

4.1. Corpora

To perform evaluation, we prepared several corpora.[10] The **Bible corpus** is the contents of a Western Armenian translation of the Bible, available from an Armenian church website.[11] The **News corpus** consists of the the contents of the Kantsasar Armenian News website from Syria.[12] Content was scraped in early November, 2021, using a web spider written using Scrapy.[13] The **Wikipedia corpus** consists of the pages and articles dump of the Western Armenian Wikipedia[14] from January 1, 2022. Text files were extracted from the XML dump.[15] We likewise tested our Western transducer over the **UD Treebank**

[8]The source URLs for these websites are listed as comments in the `.lexd` files for names. Some names were taken from Eastern Armenian sources or were written in the non-conservative orthography. These were manually adapted to Western Armenian spelling conventions.

[9]These numbers reflect the state of the transducer as of mid-January, 2022.

[10]All evaluation was performed on revision `a2ad591`, from mid-January, 2022.

[11]`https://hycatholic.ru/biblia/` The name of the translated edition is not specified, but the translation is stated as being from 1994.

[12]`http://www.kantsasar.com/news/`

[13]`https://scrapy.org/`

[14]`https://hyw.wikipedia.org/`

[15]`https://wiki.apertium.org/wiki/Wikipedia_Extractor`

for Western Armenian (in UD v2.9) (Yavrumyan et al., 2021b). The treebank included a training set, development set, and test set.

4.2. Naive coverage

Naive coverage is the number of forms in a corpus for which the analyzer returns an analysis, regardless of whether the analysis is correct or not. Ambiguity is the average number of analyses returned by the analyzer per analyzed form. Table 2 shows the naive coverage and ambiguity of the Western Armenian transducer on the corpora described in §4.1.

corpus	tokens	coverage	ambiguity
Bible	744K	99.33%	1.54
News	1.78M	95.00%	1.56
Wikipedia	3.56M	90.67%	1.37
UD training	70K	95.33%	1.44
UD dev	9.6K	96.35%	1.48
UD test	10K	96.72%	1.46

Table 2: Naive coverage on Western Armenian

Naive coverage is above 90% for all corpora, and at or above 95% for most. This level of coverage is very high, and should be considered sufficient for many tasks. Many of the top unanalyzed forms are in fact forms from other languages which should not be analyzed, especially in the Wikipedia corpus. Actual missing content in the transducer mostly consists of proper nouns and some rarely occurring stems which are not found in Armenian-English dictionaries.[16] Some tokens are also words from other Armenian dialects, such as Classical Armenian and Eastern Armenian (whether in the traditional or reformed spelling).

Ambiguity is around 1.5, meaning that there are approximately 3 analyses returned for every 2 analyzed tokens. Disambiguation is a task for future work.

4.3. Accuracy

We evaluated the precision and recall of our transducer over a random sample of words. We first retrieved 1300 random tokens from the News corpus. We then cleaned the sample by removing words that were typos, foreign words, words from other dialects or spelling systems, or were words that were so low-frequency that we couldn't find them in any modern dictionary. In all, 1225 tokens were hand-annotated. The results are shown in Table 3.

Tokens	Precision	Recall
1225	90.58%	74.82%

Table 3: Precision and recall measurements

Precision measures how many of the transducer-provided analyses for the tokens were correct. Recall measures how many of the correct analyses were retrieved from the transducer. Although our precision was high at nearly 90%, our recall rate was around 75%. This was because the transducer currently accepts more forms for a given analysis than is correct. This "overanalysis" is due to complications in the variable application of some phonological rules that are reflected in the orthography (vowel reduction), and semantically-induced variation in plural marking (§5.2). Future work would remedy this issue.

4.4. Compilation speed

One current weakness of the `lexd` compiler is compilation speed and memory use. As of revision `41b8555`, the transducer took 2 minutes 56 seconds and peak memory usage of 4.29GB to compile using a single core of an Intel i9-9900X CPU (3.50GHz). We were able to optimise many of the definitions by factoring out common subpatterns (revision `49a7487`). After this, compilation on the same system took only 48 seconds with peak memory usage of 387MB. This constitutes a nearly four-fold decrease in speed and an over 11 times decrease in memory usage.

5. Future work

This section briefly outlines our thoughts on how this transducer could be improved through increasing coverage (5.1) and handling overgeneration (5.2). Expansions to handle additional dialects which is a quite complicated problem, postponed to (6).

5.1. Increasing coverage

As stated, our lexicon was based off of a published dictionary that had at least 60k lemmas. Both the original dictionary and its digitized content had a few errors in terms of spelling or part-of-speech assignment. We tried to find as many errors as possible. Future work should go through the entire dictionary more carefully to weed out other errors. We can also cross-reference our dictionary with another dictionary in order to help find other errors or increase coverage. We are currently trying to do so with additional digitized dictionaries from Nayiri.

5.2. Handling overgeneration

One complication for our generator comes from compounds. Compounds are formed by concatenating two stems with a vowel ա /ɑ/ intervening. Compounds are listed as single orthographic words in the dictionary. For inflecting a compounds, knowing the right plural suffix depends on knowing the word's semantics (Donabédian, 2004; Dolatian, 2021). Such information cannot be easily determined from the dictionary, so without further work our generator overgenerates. To fix this issue, a possible future step is to use the lemma list of the EANC, which provides this semantic information.

6. Cross-dialectal support

It would be ideal if the current Western Armenian transducer can interface with a transducer for Eastern Armenian, cf. strategies in Vidal-Gorène et al. (2020). The two

[16] A future step would be incorporate digitized Armenian-Armenian dictionaries which can have as many as 100K lemmas.

dialects share large portions of their morphology and orthography, and code switching can be found within large corpora.

6.1. Differences between dialects

Eastern Armenian is the official language and dialect of Armenia. It has many morphological differences from Western Armenian, which are reflected in the orthography. Thus a morphological transducer for Western Armenian is not expected to work perfectly for Eastern Armenian, even when orthographic differences are accounted for.

In terms of orthography, up until the mid 20th century, Eastern Armenian in Armenia was written in the Classical Orthography system (Sanjian, 1996). This is the system that is still in use for Western Armenian. But during the Soviet era, various spelling reforms were applied to Eastern Armenian as spoken within the Soviet Union. The current spelling system is called the Reformed Orthographic system. This system applies to Eastern Armenian as spoken in Armenia and most of the Eastern Armenian diaspora. The exception is the Eastern Armenian community in Iran which still uses the Classical Orthography. Some Eastern liturgical literature is still published in the Classical Orthography.

To illustrate, in Table 4, we show the pronunciation and spelling of a passive verb 'to be gathered' for Western and Eastern Armenian. The main morphological difference is that Western Armenian uses a theme vowel ի /-i-/ for passives, while Eastern Armenian uses a theme vowel ե /-e-/. The classical spelling of the passive suffix /-v-/ is ու ‹ow›, while the reformed spelling is վ ‹v›.

		Spelling	
	Pronunciation	Traditional	Reformed
W	[kʰɑʁ-v-i-l]	քաղուիլ	—
	'gather-PASS-TH-INF'	‹k'aɣowil›	
E	[kʰɑʁ-v-e-l]	քաղուել	քաղվել
	'gather-PASS-TH-INF'	‹k'aɣowel›	‹k'aɣvel›

Table 4: Example of orthographic and morphological differences between Western (W) and Eastern (E) Armenian for the form քաղ<v><iv><pass><inf>.

6.2. Evaluating the analyzer on Eastern Armenian

For exploratory purposes, we tested our Western transducer on Eastern corpora. We found two Eastern **Bibles**. One Eastern Bible was written with the traditional orthography,[17] and one with the reformed orthography.[18] Besides orthographic differences, the two Bibles are non-identical translations, both against each other and against the Western Bible. For example, the traditional Eastern Bible used more archaic syntactic constructions, obsolete function words, and more footnotes. We also tested the transducer on pages and articles from the Eastern Armenian **Wikipedia**, from January 1 2022.[19] We likewise tested our transducer over the **UD Treebank** for Eastern Armenian (v2.9) (Yavrumyan et al., 2021a), which uses the reformed orthography. In Table 5, we report naive coverage of our Western Armenian transducer on these Eastern Armenian corpora.

corpus	spelling type	tokens	coverage
Bible	traditional	832k	93.61%
Bible	reformed	775k	79.96%
Wikipedia	reformed	62M	67.92%
UD training	reformed	42K	74.65%
UD dev	reformed	5.3K	72.44%
UD test	reformed	5.3K	74.76%
UD BSUT	reformed	3.1K	74.69%

Table 5: Naive coverage on Eastern Armenian corpora

6.2.1. High coverage on the traditional orthography

For Eastern Armenian corpora with traditional spelling, our transducer works quite well: 93% for the Eastern Bible, while 99% for the Western Bible. The high coverage rate is not surprising because the two dialects share the bulk of the same lexicon and derivational/inflectional morphology. They differ significantly in their phonology and pronunciations, but the orthography doesn't show these differences.

The fact that the two dialects have unequal naive coverage is because some inflectional suffixes are present in Eastern but not Western Armenian. Some high-frequency words likewise have different orthographic representations across the two lects. For example, the most common 'unknown' word in the traditional Eastern Bible is 'he said' at 3812 tokens. This word is [ɑsɑt͡sʰ] ասաց ‹asat͡s'› in Eastern Armenian, but [əsɑv] ըսաւ ‹əsav› in Western.

6.2.2. Low coverage on the reformed orthography

The coverage of the Western Armenian transducer over Eastern corpora with the reformed spelling is drastically lower, anywhere between 67% to 79% percent. This difference is likely because of rampant spelling differences across the two spelling systems. For example, the most common 'unknown' word over the reformed Eastern Bible is the word [jev] 'and' at 4026 tokens. This word is spelled as եւ ‹ew› in the traditional system (in both Western and Eastern Armenian) but եվ or և ‹ev› in the reformed system. The reformed Bible that we used almost always used the եվ form.

6.3. Combining the dialects in one analyzer

There are several ways that the transducer could be expanded to support multiple dialects. We have already be-

[17] http://ter-hambardzum.net/armenia-bible-online/

[18] https://hycatholic.ru/biblio/աստվածաշունչ/

[19] The Wikipedia (https://hy.wikipedia.org/) is primarily written in Eastern with the reformed orthography, but there are some articles in Western or in the traditional orthography.

gun expanding the transducer source code and compilation instructions in one such way. When not the same across dialects, stems and inflectional morphology may be specified on a per-dialect level. This allows the compilation of separate analyzers, separate generators, and a combined analyzer.

7. Conclusions

This paper overviewed the development of a free/open-source morphological analyzer and generator for Western Armenian. In terms of naive coverage, it performs quite well over various Western Armenian corpora. It has high precision and okay recall. It likewise has some coverage over other dialects, thus paving the way for creating a pan-dialectal transducer.

8. Bibliographical References

Adjarian, H. (1909). *Classification des dialectes arméniens*. Librairie Honoré Champion, Paris.

Al-Bataineh, A. (2015). *Cent ans après: Politiques scolaires et la vitalité des langues en danger le cas de l'arménien occidental*. Ph.D. thesis, Sorbonne Paris Cité.

Arakelyan, G., Hambardzumyan, K., and Khachatrian, H. (2018). Towards JointUD: Part-of-speech tagging and lemmatization using recurrent neural networks. In *Proceedings of the CoNLL 2018 Shared Task: Multilingual Parsing from Raw Text to Universal Dependencies*, pages 180–186, Brussels, Belgium, October. Association for Computational Linguistics.

Arkhangelskiy, T., Belyaev, O., and Vydrin, A. (2012). The creation of large-scale annotated corpora of minority languages using UniParser and the EANC platform. In *Proceedings of COLING 2012: Posters*, pages 83–92.

Beesley, K. and Karttunen, L. (2003). *Finite-state morphology: Xerox tools and techniques*. CSLI Publications, Stanford, CA.

Boyacioglu, N. (2010). *Hay-Pay: Les Verbs de l'arménien occidental*. L'Asiatheque, Paris.

Chahinian, T. and Bakalian, A. (2016). Language in Armenian American communities: Western Armenian and efforts for preservation. *International Journal of the Sociology of Language*, 2016(237):37–57.

Chiarcos, C., Donandt, K., Ionov, M., Rind-Pawlowski, M., Sargsian, H., Wichers Schreur, J., Abromeit, F., and Fäth, C. (2018). Universal Morphologies for the Caucasus region. In *Proceedings of the Eleventh International Conference on Language Resources and Evaluation (LREC 2018)*, Miyazaki, Japan, May. European Language Resources Association (ELRA).

Cowe, S. P. (1992). Amēn teł hay kay: Armenian as a pluricentric language. In Michael Clyne, editor, *Pluricentric Languages: Differing Norms in Different Nations*, pages 325–346. De Gruyter Mouton.

Dolatian, H. (2021). The role of heads and cyclicity in bracketing paradoxes in Armenian compounds. *Morphology*, 31(1):1–43.

Donabédian, A. and Boyacioglu, N. (2007). La lemmatisation de l'arménien occidental avec nooj. In Svetla Koeva, et al., editors, *Formaliser les langues avec l'ordinateur: De INTEX à NooJ*, Cahiers de la MSH Ledoux, pages 55–76. Presses Universitaires de Franche-Comté, France.

Donabédian, A. (2004). Le nom composé en arménien. In Pierre J.L. Arnaud, editor, *Le nom composé: Données sur seize langues*, pages 3–20. Presses Universitaires de Lyon, Lyon.

Donabédian, A. (2018). Middle east and beyond - Western Armenian at the crossroads: A sociolinguistic and typological sketch. In Christiane Bulut, editor, *Linguistic minorities in Turkey and Turkic-speaking minorities of the periphery*, pages 89–148. Harrazowitz Verlag, Wiesbaden.

Dum-Tragut, J. (2009). *Armenian: Modern Eastern Armenian*. Number 14 in London Oriental and African Language Library. John Benjamins Publishing Company, Amsterdam/Philadelphia.

David M. Eberhard, et al., editors. (2022). *Ethnologue: Languages of the World*. SIL International, Dallas, Texas, online, twenty-fifth edition.

Ghukasyan, T., Davtyan, G., Avetisyan, K., and Andrianov, I. (2018). pioNER: Datasets and baselines for Armenian named entity recognition. In *2018 Ivannikov Ispras Open Conference (ISPRAS)*, pages 56–61. IEEE.

Hagopian, G. (2005). *Armenian for everyone: Western and Eastern Armenian in parallel lessons*. Caravan Books, Ann Arbor, MI.

Jebejian, A. (2007). *Changing ideologies and extralinguistic determinants in language maintenance and shift among ethnic diaspora Armenians in Beirut*. Ph.D. thesis, University of Leicester.

Karttunen, L. (2006). The insufficiency of paper-and-pencil linguistics: The case of Finnish prosody. In Miriam Butt, et al., editors, *Intelligent linguistic architectures: Variations on themes by Ronald M. Kaplan*, number 179 in CSLI Lecture Notes, pages 287–300. CSLI, Stanford, CA.

Khachatryan, L. (2012). Formalization of proper names in the Western Armenian press. In Kristina Vučković, et al., editors, *Formalising Natural Languages with NooJ: Selected Papers from the NooJ 2011 International Conference (Dubrovnik, Croatia)*, pages 75–85. Cambridge Scholars Publishing, Newcastle, UK.

Khachatryan, L. (2013). An Armenian grammar for proper names. In Anaïd Donabédian, et al., editors, *Formalising Natural Languages with NooJ: Selected Papers from the NooJ 2012 International Conference (Paris, France)*, pages 233–234. Cambridge Scholars Publishing, Newcastle, UK.

Khurshudian, V. G., Daniel, M. A., Levonian, D. V., Plungian, V. A., Polyakov, A. E., and Rubakov, S. A. (2009). Eastern Armenian National Corpus. In *Computational Linguistics and Intellectual Technologies (Papers from the Annual International Conference*

"*Dialogue 2009*", volume 8, pages 509–518, Moscow. RGGU.

Kirov, C., Cotterell, R., Sylak-Glassman, J., Walther, G., Vylomova, E., Xia, P., Faruqui, M., Mielke, S. J., McCarthy, A., Kübler, S., Yarowsky, D., Eisner, J., and Hulden, M. (2018). UniMorph 2.0: Universal Morphology. In *Proceedings of the Eleventh International Conference on Language Resources and Evaluation (LREC 2018)*, Miyazaki, Japan, May. European Language Resources Association (ELRA).

Koskenniemi, K. (1984). A general computational model for word-form recognition and production. In *Proceedings of the 10th international conference on Computational Linguistics*, pages 178–181. Association for Computational Linguistics.

Kouyoumdjian, M. G. (1970). *A comprehensive dictionary, Armenian-English*. Atlas Press, Beirut.

Lindén, K., Axelson, E., Hardwick, S., Pirinen, T. A., and Silfverberg, M. (2011). Hfst—framework for compiling and applying morphologies. In *International Workshop on Systems and Frameworks for Computational Morphology*, pages 67–85. Springer.

Lonsdale, D. and Danielyan, I. (2004). A two-level implementation for western Armenian morphology. *Annual of Armenian linguistics*, 24:35–51.

McCarthy, A. D., Kirov, C., Grella, M., Nidhi, A., Xia, P., Gorman, K., Vylomova, E., Mielke, S. J., Nicolai, G., Silfverberg, M., Arkhangelskiy, T., Krizhanovsky, N., Krizhanovsky, A., Klyachko, E., Sorokin, A., Mansfield, J., Ernštreits, V., Pinter, Y., Jacobs, C. L., Cotterell, R., Hulden, M., and Yarowsky, D. (2020). UniMorph 3.0: Universal Morphology. In *Proceedings of The 12th Language Resources and Evaluation Conference*, pages 3922–3931, Marseille, France, May. European Language Resources Association.

Megerdoomian, K. (2009). Low-density language strategies for persian and Armenian. In Sergei Nirenburg, editor, *Language Engineering for Lesser-Studied Languages*, pages 291–312. IOS Press, Amsterdam.

Roark, B. and Sproat, R. (2007). *Computational Approaches to Morphology and Syntax*. Oxford University Press, Oxford.

Sanjian, A. K. (1996). The Armenian alphabet. In Peter T. Daniels et al., editors, *The World's Writing Systems*, pages 356–357. Oxford University Press, New York and Oxford.

Sayeed, O. and Vaux, B. (2017). The evolution of Armenian. In Jared S Klein, et al., editors, *Handbook of Comparative and Historical Indo-European Linguistics*, pages 1146–1167. Walter de Gruyter, Berlin/Boston.

Silberztein, M. (2016). *Formalizing Natural Languages: The NooJ Approach*. ISTE LTd and John Wiley & Sons, London and Hoboken, NJ.

Skopeteas, S., Hovhannisyan, H., and Brokmann, C. (2015). Eastern Armenian spoken corpus.

Swanson, D. and Howell, N. (2021). Lexd: A finite-state lexicon compiler for non-suffixational morphologies. In Mika Hämäläinen, et al., editors, *Multilingual Facilitation*, pages 133–146. Helsingin yliopisto.

Vidal-Gorène, C. and Decours-Perez, A. (2020). Languages resources for poorly endowed languages : The case study of Classical Armenian. In *Proceedings of The 12th Language Resources and Evaluation Conference*, pages 3145–3152, Marseille, France, May. European Language Resources Association.

Vidal-Gorène, C. and Kindt, B. (2020). Lemmatization and POS-tagging process by using joint learning approach. experimental results on Classical Armenian, Old Georgian, and Syriac. In *Proceedings of LT4HALA 2020 - 1st Workshop on Language Technologies for Historical and Ancient Languages*, pages 22–27, Marseille, France, May. European Language Resources Association (ELRA).

Vidal-Gorène, C., Khurshudyan, V., and Donabédian-Demopoulos, A. (2020). Recycling and comparing morphological annotation models for Armenian diachronic-variational corpus processing. In *Proceedings of the 7th Workshop on NLP for Similar Languages, Varieties and Dialects*, pages 90–101.

Yavrumyan, M. M., Khachatrian, H. H., Danielyan, A. S., and Arakelyan, G. D. (2017). ArmTDP: Eastern Armenian Treebank and Dependency Parser. In *XI International Conference on Armenian Linguistics, Abstracts*, Yerevan.

Yavrumyan, M. M. (2019). Universal dependencies for Armenian. Presented at the International Conference on Digital Armenian, Inalco, Paris, October 3-5.

Zhang, H., Sproat, R., Ng, A. H., Stahlberg, F., Peng, X., Gorman, K., and Roark, B. (2019). Neural models of text normalization for speech applications. *Computational Linguistics*, 45(2):293–337.

9. Language Resource References

Nisan Boyacioglu and Hossep Dolatian. (2020). *Armenian Verbs: Paradigms and verb lists of Western Armenian conjugation classes (v.1.0.0)*. Zenodo.

Marat M. Yavrumyan and Hrant H. Khachatrian and Anna S. Danielyan and Gor D. Arakelyan and Martin S. Mirakyan and Liana G. Minasyan. (2021a). *UD Eastern Armenian ArmTDP*. In *Universal Dependencies 2.9*, ed. Zeman, D., J. Nivre, et al.

Marat M. Yavrumyan and Hrant H. Khachatrian and Anna S. Danielyan and Setrag H.M. Hovsepian and Liana G. Minasyan. (2021b). *UD Western Armenian ArmTDP*. In *Universal Dependencies 2.9*, ed. Zeman, D., J. Nivre, et al.

Proceedings of the Workshop on Processing Language Variation: Digital Armenian (DigitAm 2022) @LREC2022, pages 8–12
Marseille, 20 June 2022

Dialects Identification of Armenian Language

Karen Avetisyan
Russian-Armenian University
Yerevan, Armenia
avetisyan.karen@student.rau.am

Abstract

The Armenian language has many dialects that differ from each other syntactically, morphologically, and phonetically. In this work, we implement and evaluate models that determine the dialect of a given passage of text. The proposed models are evaluated for the three major variations of the Armenian language: Eastern, Western, and Classical. Previously, there were no instruments of dialect identification in the Armenian language. The paper presents three approaches: a statistical which relies on a stop words dictionary, a modified statistical one with a dictionary of most frequently encountered words, and the third one that is based on Facebook's fastText language identification neural network model. Two types of neural network models were trained, one with the usage of pre-trained word embeddings and the other without. Approaches were tested on sentence-level and document-level data. The results show that the neural network-based method works sufficiently better than the statistical ones, achieving almost 98% accuracy at the sentence level and nearly 100% at the document level.

Keywords: Dialect identification, Western Armenian, Eastern Armenian, Classical Armenian

1. Introduction

The Armenian language has many actively used dialects. They differ from each other syntactically, morphologically, and phonetically. Considering the variation in the existing literature and the current usage of various variants of the language, dialect identification in texts is a relevant and open problem for Armenian dialects. Thus, this paper tries to solve that problem for three major variations of the Armenian language: Eastern, Western, and Classical.

Dialect identification is similar to language identification, but has several important differences that make the task more challenging. Contrary to different languages, dialects share the same script and have highly overlapping vocabularies. Despite the subtle differences between the tasks, to solve the dialect identification task in this work we study the performance of established lexicon- and artificial neural network-based language identification approaches.

Lexicon-based methods use a list of stop words for each language to detect their texts. A similar approach was shown in Truică et al. (2015), where the stop words and diacritics formed the lexicon. The Armenian language has no diacritics and stop words can be very similar among dialects, therefore this method may not always be suitable for the chosen task. For that reason, it was modified to use the list of the most frequent words of each of the considered dialects.

The artificial neural network-based approach learns numerical representations of words and uses them as input features for classification. One of the most popular implementations of this method relies on Facebook's fastText library[1] for text classification and representation (Joulin et al., 2016) as it has shown high results on language identification tasks. Here, the model was trained both with the usage of the pre-trained fastText word embeddings and without it. To train the model, data from Western[2] and Eastern[3] Armenian Wikipedia was collected, as well as the data from Digilib[4] for Classical Armenian.

All three methods were tested on sentence-level and document-level testing datasets that were also collected from Wikipedia-s and Digilib texts. In addition to this, the dependency of text segment size to dialect identification accuracy is shown.

2. Methods

To solve the task of Armenian dialect identification, three methods were used.

(i) Stop Words: As a baseline solution for the problem, a stop-word-based algorithm was selected. Let W_d be the stop words vocabulary of the dialect $d(d \in \{Western, Eastern, Classical\})$. W_e is the set of words contained in the text E. For each text E, the dialect is predicted according to this statement:

$$label(E) = argmax_d\ (|W_d \cap W_e|)$$

If there are two or three maximal values, the label is chosen randomly according to the values.

(ii) Lexicon-Based: The first method was modified by making the W_d not only stop words vocabulary. Here, 2 different W_d vocabularies were tested. The process of both W_d dictionary-formation is described in Chapter 3.

(iii) Neural Network-Based: For the other method, Facebook's fastText language identification model was utilized. Here, the words are being presented as a set of n-grams. Each n-gram has its representation vector that is also trainable. These representations are then being averaged and given to a linear classifier. In the end, *softmax* is used as an activation function.

The model was trained to predict 3 dialects: Eastern Armenian, Western Armenian, and Classical Armenian.

[1] https://fasttext.cc/blog/2017/10/02/blog-post.html
[2] https://hyw.wikipedia.org/
[3] https://hy.wikipedia.org/
[4] https://digilib.aua.am/en

3. Data

To collect the training data for Eastern (hye) and Western (hyw) Armenian, respective Wikipedia dumps[5][6] were used. Whereas, the texts from Digilib were utilized to get the data for Classical Armenian.
The stop word dictionary for Western and Classical Armenian was collected manually utilizing the list of most frequent words that was in turn collected from the above-described resources. Eastern Armenian stop words were taken from here[7].
For the lexicon-based method, three dictionaries (one for each dialect) were formed. The formation was processed, in two different ways, using the corresponding data for each of the dialects separately. Removing the words that contain non-Armenian letters as well as punctuation symbols, the word frequency was counted. Assuming that $\boldsymbol{V_{A,k}}$ stands for the set of top k most frequent words in dialect A, the final dictionary for the dialect A, in two different ways **a)** and **b)**, will look as follows:

$$\text{a)} \quad D_A = V_{A,k} \setminus (V_{B,k} \cap V_{C,k}),$$
$$\text{b)} \quad D_A = V_{A,k} \setminus (V_{B,k} \cup V_{C,k}),$$

where $\boldsymbol{V_{B,k}}$ and $\boldsymbol{V_{C,k}}$ are the sets of top k frequent words in dialects B and C, respectively.
As for the data to train the fastText language identification model, sentences were randomly extracted from the considered datasets. It was decided not to filter the extracted sentences according to their length, taking into account the fact that fastText trains its own models using sentences with different lengths. For each of the dialects, the training set contains an equal number of sentences.
To test the methods, two types of test data were created. The first one is a set of sentences randomly extracted from the Wikipedia dumps and Digilib. For each dialect, this set contains 500 sentences. The average length of the sentences is equal to nearly 18 words or ≈ 130 characters.
The second test set consists of whole texts, a hundred documents for each dialect, randomly extracted from the same sources. The average length of the document is equal to ≈ 600 words or ≈ 4150 characters. For Classical Armenian, only the first 50 sentences of each document were extracted to balance the average length of documents for each of the dialects.

4. Experiments

In this chapter, the process of hyperparameter tuning, the results on tuned hyperparameters, and some other additional statistics are shown.
The best results that each of the described methods achieve, and their corresponding time consumption, are shown in Table 1 and Table 2 separately for sentence and document level test sets.
According to the results shown in Table 1 and Table 2, the neural network-based method achieves sufficiently better results than the ones based on vocabulary.
Further, in subchapters 4.1 and 4.2 more detailed results for all the conducted experiments are described.

Methods	Accuracy	Time
Stop-Words	0.51	0.02s
Lexicon-Based	0.67	1.71s
Neural-Network	0.98	0.14s

Table 1: The best results and time consumption of each method on the **sentence-level test set**.
(Processing time of 1500 sentence examples)

Methods	Accuracy	Time
Stop-Words	0.55	0.04s
Lexicon-Based	0.67	0.16s
Neural Network	1.00	0.76s

Table 2: The best results and time consumption of each method on the **document-level test set**.
(Processing time of 300 document examples)

4.1 Lexicon-based method

For the lexicon-based method, we tuned k, the number of the most frequent words used to create the final dictionaries. For each value of k, and for both variations of dictionary-creation, the accuracy score was calculated. The results of these experiments for sentence-level and document-level test sets are shown in Figure 1 and Figure 2.

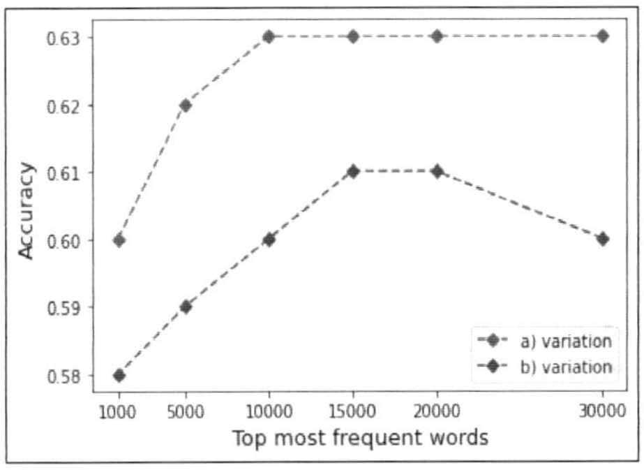

Figure 1: The comparison of a) and b) dictionary versions in terms of accuracy score shown on the **sentence-level** test set depending on the number of most frequent words taken.

According to the results (Figure 1 and Figure 2), it is noticeable that the **b)** version of dictionary-creation overall works better on both of the test sets.

4.2 Neural network-based method

For this method, we trained the fastText model on 3 different size datasets. These datasets consisted of 1000, 2000, and 5000 sentences per each label.

[5] https://dumps.wikimedia.org/hywwiki/
[6] https://dumps.wikimedia.org/hywiki/
[7] https://github.com/stopwords-iso/stopwords-hy

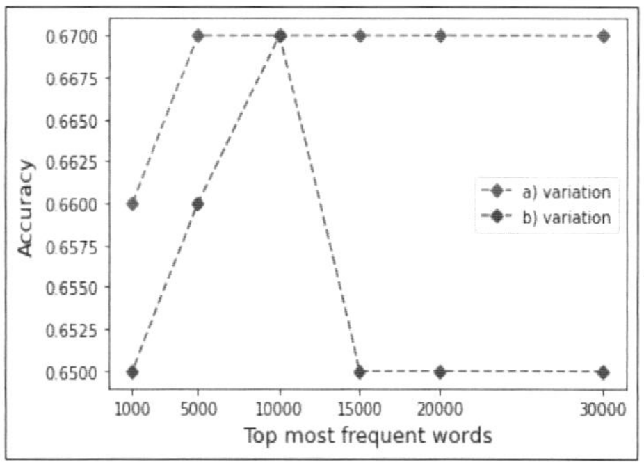

Figure 2: The comparison of a) and b) dictionary versions in terms of accuracy score shown on the **document-level** test set depending on the number of most frequent words taken.

4.2.1 Hyperparameters

For more efficient usage of the method, we had to tune some basic hyperparameters like *minn* and *maxn,* which denote the minimal and maximal length of character n-grams. Taking into account the fact that the average length of the words used in the training set is nearly 6 characters, the minimal and maximal lengths of character n-grams were tuned within these limits.

In addition, the process of training was held with and without pre-trained word vectors. While using the pre-trained word vectors, the *dim* parameter, which stands for the size of word vectors, was equal to 300. As pre-trained word vectors, fastText's default vectors for the Armenian language were used. When the training process was held without pre-trained vectors, the *dim* parameter was set to 16 as it is suggested in the fastTexts language identification tutorial[8].

Hyperparameter tuning was performed on the sentence-level test set. The results both with and without the usage of pre-trained word vectors are shown in Table 3 and Table 4. The presented results are the average of 5 separate runs with different random seeds.

As we can see from Table 3 and Table 4, the results are much more stable with the usage of pre-trained vectors, while the n-gram minimum and maximum sizes change. The best results were also achieved with the usage of pre-trained vectors with the training set size of 5000 sentences per label.

4.2.2 Results

Based on the hyperparameter tuning results, the models that achieved the best results were taken. For these models, their confusion matrixes are presented in Figure 3. As we can see from these matrixes, the models are mainly confused in predicting Classical Armenian sentences as Western Armenian ones, and Western Armenian sentences as Eastern Armenian ones.

Sentences per label	1000						2000						5000					
maxn / minn	1	2	3	4	5	6	1	2	3	4	5	6	1	2	3	4	5	6
1	93,3	95,7	96	**96,1**	96	95,9	94,1	96,2	96,9	**97,1**	97	97	95,2	96,7	96,7	96,9	97,2	97,1
2		95,3	95,4	95,7	95,7	95,8		96,3	97	97	97	97		96,3	96,5	97	97,1	97,3
3			95,5	95,5	95,5	95,5			96,7	96,9	96,9	96,9			97	97,5	**97,6**	97,5
4				95,2	94,9	94,7				96,9	96,9	96,9				96,9	97,2	97,3
5					94,4	94,2					96,7	96,7					96,7	96,9
6						94,1						96,6						96,6

Table 3: *minn* and *maxn* hyperparameters tuning, on sentence-level test set, for different size training data **with** pre-trained word vectors (dim=300).

Sentences per label	1000						2000						5000					
maxn / minn	1	2	3	4	5	6	1	2	3	4	5	6	1	2	3	4	5	6
1	84,4	74,9	71,4	76,2	81,6	68,9	90,1	94,2	93,4	91,7	89,7	83,2	92,7	96	96,1	96,1	96	95,9
2		**88,7**	68,6	73,4	79,7	77,8		**94,8**	94,1	92,9	91,1	84,5		96,1	96,7	96,5	96,4	96,3
3			85,2	74	78,7	78,9			94,6	93,6	90,9	81,2			**97**	96,9	96,4	96,1
4				79,1	76,8	72,9				94,3	92,2	85,5				96,5	96,4	96
5					71,7	61,3					92,8	89					96,2	96,1
6						68,1						91,9						95,9

Table 4: *minn* and *maxn* hyperparameters tuning, on sentence-level test set, for different size training data **without** pre-trained word vectors (dim=16).

[8] https://fasttext.cc/blog/2017/10/02/blog-post.html

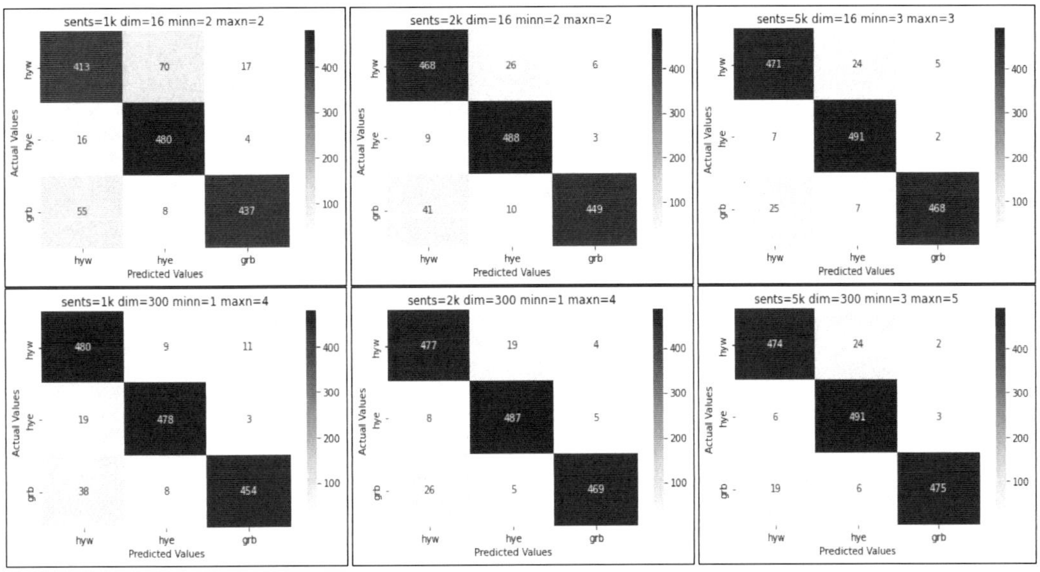

Figure 3: Confusion matrixes of models with best hyperparameters on the sentence-level test set.

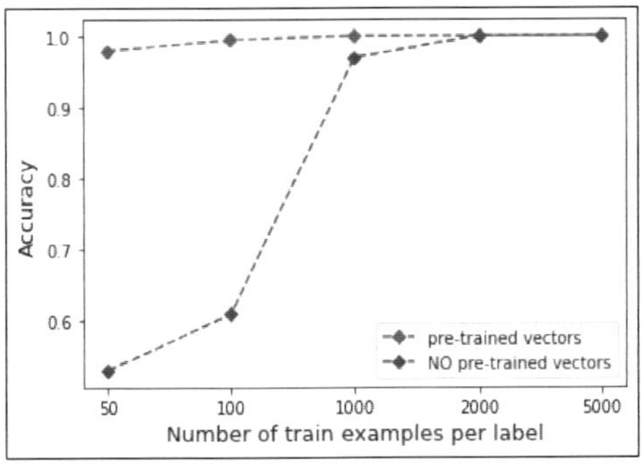

Figure 4: A comparison of models that were trained with and without pre-trained vectors on the **document-level test set**, while changing the number of training examples.

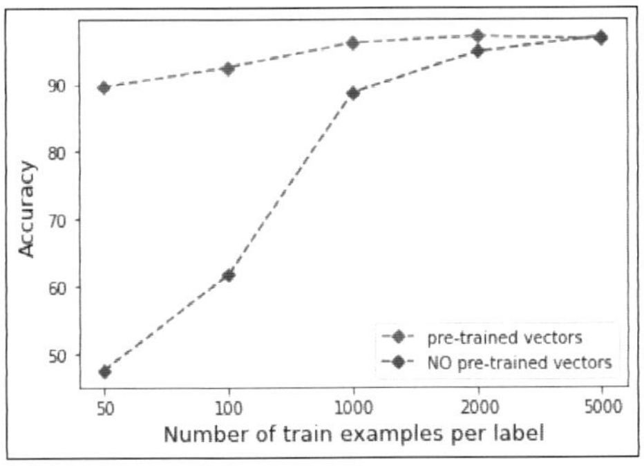

Figure 5: A comparison of models that were trained with and without pre-trained vectors on the **sentence-level test set**, while changing the number of training examples.

The best models for each number of train examples and according to the usage of pre-trained vectors were also tested on the sentence and document level test sets. These results are shown in Figure 4 and Figure 5. Here the presented results are also the average of 5 seeds.

From Figure 4 and Figure 5 we can conclude that the models for which pre-trained vectors were used achieve the same results with a smaller amount of data used for their training. Also, we can see that the model that does not use pre-trained vectors and for the training of which 5000 sentences per label were used, achieves nearly the same results as the model that uses the vectors.

Further, to minimize the time consumption on the document-level dialect identification task, additional experiments were held using only the first n symbols of each test example. The value of n was changed from 10 to 200 symbols. Time consumption for an experiment, where n was equal to 200 symbols, was decreased by nearly 20 times for each of the considered models. The achieved accuracy scores for these experiments are shown in Figure 6. The final scores were also calculated by averaging the results of 5 seeds.

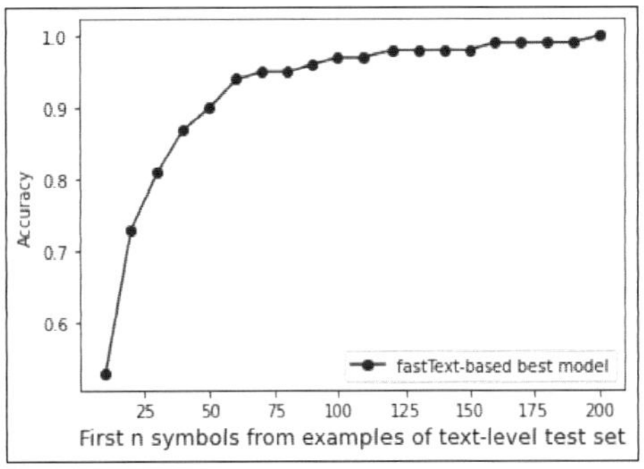

Figure 6: Accuracy score according to the change of a number of first symbols that are given to the neural network-based best model.

5. Conclusion

In this work, we evaluated three different methods of Armenian dialect identification. The neural network-based method performed best, achieving 98% accuracy at sentence level and 100% accuracy at document level. Utilizing pre-trained word vectors to train the neural network allowed us to achieve decent results for this task, using only a small number of training examples. This feature could be helpful for the identification process of less popular dialects. Additionally, it was shown that using only the first 200 characters of the document would be sufficient for accurate dialect identification, which in practice will help to significantly reduce the computation time when processing long documents.

6. Bibliographical References

Ali, A., Dehak, N., Cardinal, P., Khurana, S., Yella, S., Glass, J., Bell, P. and Renals, S. (2016). Automatic Dialect Detection in Arabic Broadcast Speech. *Interspeech 2016.*

Balaji, N.N.A. and Bharathi B. (2020). Semi-supervised Fine-grained Approach for Arabic dialect detection task. *In Proceedings of the Fifth Arabic Natural Language Processing Workshop*, pages 257–261, Barcelona, Spain.

Belinkov, Y. & Glass, J. (2016). A Character-level Convolutional Neural Network for Distinguishing Similar Languages and Dialects. *VarDial@COLING.*

Biadsy, F., Hirschberg, J. and Habash, N. (2009). Spoken Arabic Dialect Identification Using Phonotactic Modeling. *Proceedings of EACL 2009 Workshop on Computational Approaches to Semitic Languages.*

Darwish, K., Sajjad, H., & Mubarak, H. (2014). Verifiably effective arabic dialect identification. *In Proceedings of the 2014 Conference on Empirical Methods in Natural Language Processing (EMNLP),* pages 1465-1468.

Franco-Penya, H.-H. and Sanchez, L.M. (2016). Tuning Bayes Baseline for Dialect Detection. *In Proceedings of the Third Workshop on NLP for Similar Languages, Varieties and Dialects (VarDial3),* pages 227–234, Osaka, Japan.

Joulin, A., Grave, E., Bojanowski, P. and Mikolov, T. (2016). Bag of Tricks for Efficient Text Classification. *Proceedings of the 15th Conference of the European Chapter of the Association for Computational Linguistics: Volume 2, Short Papers.*

Malmasi, S., Refaee, E. and Dras, M. (2015). Arabic Dialect Identification Using a Parallel Multidialectal Corpus. *PACLING 2015.*

Talafha, B., Ali, M., Za'ter, M. E., Seelawi, H., Tuffaha, I., Samir, M., Farhan W. & Al-Natsheh, H. T. (2020). Multi-dialect arabic bert for country-level dialect identification.

Truică, C.-O., Velcin, J. and Boicea, A. (2015). Automatic Language Identification for Romance Languages Using Stop Words and Diacritics. 17th *International Symposium on Symbolic and Numeric Algorithms for Scientific Computing.*

Proceedings of the Workshop on Processing Language Variation: Digital Armenian (DigitAm 2022) @LREC2022, pages 13–20
Marseille, 20 June 2022

Analyse Automatique de l'Arménien Ancien. Évaluation d'une méthode hybride « dictionnaire » et « réseau de neurones » sur un Extrait de l'*Adversus Haereses* d'Irénée de Lyon

Gabriel Kepeklian, Bastien Kindt
Centre d'études orientales – Institut orientaliste de Louvain (CIOL),
Institut des civilisations, arts et lettres (INCAL),
UCLouvain, Louvain-la-Neuve, Belgium
{gabriel.kepeklian,bastien.kindt}@uclouvain.be

Abstract

The aim of this paper is to evaluate a lexical analysis (mainly lemmatization and POS-tagging) of a sample of the Ancient Armenian version of the *Adversus Haereses* by Irenaeus of Lyons (2nd c.) by using hybrid approach based on digital dictionaries on the one hand, and on Recurrent Neural Network (RNN) on the other hand. The quality of the results is checked by comparing data obtained by implementing these two methods with data manually checked. In the present case, 98,37% of the results are correct by using the first (lexical) approach, and 74,64% by using the second (RNN). But, in fact, both methods present advantages and disadvantages and argue for the hybrid method. The linguistic resources implemented here are jointly developed and tested by GREgORI and Calfa.

Mots-clés : arménien ancien, lemmatisation, étiquetage morphosyntaxique (POS-tagging), réseau de neurones (RNN)

1. Introduction

1.1 Irénée de Lyon et l'*Adversus Haereses*

Irénée (mort vers 202 ap. J.-C.) est le deuxième évêque de Lyon (Lugdunum), capitale des trois Gaules, territoires alors soumis à l'Empire romain. Père de l'Église, il est aussi considéré comme le premier théologien. Natif de Smyrne en Asie Mineure, sa langue et sa culture sont grecques. Son œuvre principale, écrite en grec, est une *Présentation et réfutation de la gnose au faut nom* (*Ἔλεγχος ἀνατροπὴ τῆς ψευδωνύμου γνώσεως*), en cinq livres. L'auteur y réfute les doctrines gnostiques venues d'Asie Mineure, puis y développe une riche pensée théologique (Rousseau, 1984). Ce texte est perdu, mais deux traductions sont parvenues jusqu'à nous. La première est une traduction latine (IVe-Ve s.) transmise sous le titre (réducteur) d'*Adversus Haereses* (« Contre les Hérésies » ; désormais *AH*). La seconde est une traduction arménienne (VIIe s.) intitulée *Յանդիմանութեան եւ եղծման ստանուն գիտութեանն Yandimanut'ean ew ełcman stanun gitut'eann* (« Présentation et réfutation de la gnose au faux nom », traduction du titre grec) connue par un unique manuscrit du XIIIe s., conservé au Maténadaran à Erevan sous la cote M3710. De nombreux fragments grecs et arméniens, et quelques autres latins et syriaques complètent en outre ces deux traductions. Le cinquième livre de l'*AH*, dans sa version arménienne, vient de faire l'objet d'une nouvelle édition par (Kepeklian, 2021)[1]. L'analyse lexicale de ce texte est en cours dans le cadre du projet GREgORI[2]. Le présent article porte sur un extrait de ce livre V qui s'étend de la préface au chapitre II, 3. Le tableau 1 indique le nombre de mots-occurrences et le nombre de formes différente dans l'ensemble du livre V et, pour l'extrait, qui est déjà analysé, le nombre de lemmes.

	Mots-occurrences (tokens)	Formes de mots (unique token)	Lemmes
Livre V	25.544	6.069	(en cours d'analyse)
Préface - Ch. II, 3	1.530	756	444

Tableau 1 : Nombre de mots-occurrences, de formes de mots et de lemmes dans l'*AH*, V et dans l'extrait (Préface - Ch. II, 3)

1.2 L'analyse de l'extrait de l'*AH* et les ressources linguistiques du projet GREgORI pour l'arménien ancien

À terme, l'analyse du livre V de l'*AH* fournira aux chercheurs un corpus entièrement étiqueté de ce texte. Ce corpus sera accessible en ligne via les interfaces du projet GREgORI[3]. Cette analyse comprend la lemmatisation de tous les mots du corpus ainsi que leur étiquetage morphosyntaxique (POS) et flexionnel. Deux méthodologies sont adoptées pour réaliser la lemmatisation et les étiquetages. 1) Une première approche compare le vocabulaire du texte aux lexiques de référence des ressources linguistiques du projet GREgORI. 2) Une seconde approche utilise un réseau de neurones préparé par Calfa[4]. Cette démarche hybride alliant une approche dite « par dictionnaires » et une approche ayant recours à l'« intelligence artificielle » est désormais privilégiée pour l'analyse

[1] Cette nouvelle édition sera publiée dans le *Corpus Scriptorum Christianorum Orientalium* édité par Peeters Publishers (Leuven, Belgique).

[2] Sur le projet GREgORI mené à l'Institut orientaliste de l'UCLouvain, sous la direction du professeur Bernard Coulie, cfr https://uclouvain.be/fr/instituts-recherche/incal/ciol/gregori-project.html.

[3] https://www.gregoriproject.com.

[4] https://calfa.fr.

des textes arméniens, géorgiens, grecs et syriaques traités dans le cadre du projet GREgORI (Vidal-Gorène and Kindt, 2020 ; Vidal-Gorène and Kindt, 2022 ; Kindt, Vidal-Gorène et Delle Donne, 2022). Pour le moment, seule la première des deux approches, celle par « par dictionnaires », fournit les analyses flexionnelles.

1.2.1 Les lexiques de référence

Comme l'illustre le tableau 2, les ressources lexicales du projet GREgORI pour l'arménien sont réunies dans des lexiques de référence totalisant 1.199.123 formes de mots, regroupées sous 30.311 lemmes.

Formes simples	315.952
Formes composées	883.171
Nombre total de formes	1.199.123
Lemmes	30.311

Tableau 2 : Nombre de lemmes, de formes simples et de formes composées enregistrées dans les ressources linguistiques du projet GREgORI

Ces ressources distinguent les formes dites « simples » (1) et les formes dites « composées » (2).

1) մարդ *mard* « homme », lemme մարդ, catégorie morphosyntaxique N+Com (nom commun), analyses flexionnelles :As:Ns:Us (accusatif singulier, nominatif singulier et locatif singulier) (les étiquettes morphosyntaxiques et flexionnelles sont énumérées dans les tableaux les annexes 3 et 4, cfr 7.3 et 7.4).

2) զմարդն *zmardn* « les hommes », segmenté lors de l'analyse en զ-մարդ-ն, I+Prep (préfixe prépositionnel), N+Com (nom commun) et PRO+Dem (suffixe déterminatif), :As (accusatif singulier)[5].

La distinction établie entre formes simples et formes composées, et donc la discrimination des préfixes prépositionnels et des suffixes déterminatifs, permet d'inclure ces éléments lexicaux dans les analyses. Ces éléments peuvent donc servir d'arguments dans les requêtes formulées par les chercheurs explorant le corpus. Les principes de formulation des intitulés de lemme et les étiquettes morphosyntaxiques et flexionnelles sont décrits dans (Coulie, Kindt, Kepeklian et Van Elverdinghe, 2022).

Mots-occurrences (tokens)	73.211
Formes simples	61.291
Formes composées	11.920
Formes de mots (unique tokens)	17.554
Formes simples	11.851
Formes composées	5.703
Lemmes	5.649

Tableau 3 : Effectifs des formes effectivement attestées dans les textes déjà traités

Les formes enregistrées dans les ressources sont soit des formes effectivement attestées dans le corpus complet des textes déjà traités dans le cadre du projet – ensemble textuel décrit dans (Vidal-Gorène, Ch. and Kindt, 2020 ; le tableau 3 en indique les effectifs) –, soit des formes générées automatiquement avec une supervision par un expert humain, comme expliqué dans (Coulie, Kindt, Kepeklian, et Van Elverdinghe, 2022).

1.2.2 Le réseau de neurones

L'approche par réseau de neurones est basée sur un apprentissage mis en œuvre sur le corpus des textes déjà traités. Elle a déjà été testée et évaluée, en arménien comme dans d'autres langues de l'Orient chrétien (Vidal-Gorène and Kindt, 2020 ; Vidal-Gorène and Kindt, 2022). Le tableau 4 rappelle les résultats obtenus à cette occasion sur un corpus de test. Sur l'ensemble des mots du corpus de test, l'*accuracy* atteint 0.9044 pour la lemmatisation et 0.9238 pour l'étiquetage morpho-syntaxique (résultats de mai 2020). Pour rappel, cette approche ne fournit pas encore les informations flexionnelles. Deux constats ont été établis lors de cette évaluation : 1) les résultats observés sont meilleurs sur les formes ambiguës que sur les formes inconnues ; 2) les résultats sont meilleurs pour la catégorisation morphosyntaxique que pour la lemmatisation.

	Toutes les formes (tokens)	Formes ambiguës (tokens)	Formes inconnues (tokens)
Lemmatisation			
accuracy	0.9044	0.8620	0.6864
precision	0.6630	0.4411	0.5074
recall	0.6711	0.5211	0.5118
f1-score	0.6670	0.4778	0.5096
Étiquetage morphosyntaxique			
accuracy	0.9238	0.9145	0.7441
precision	0.6513	0.6306	0.2920
recall	0.6264	0.6501	0.3124
f1-score	0.6386	0.6402	0.3019

Tableau 4 : Résultats de la lemmatisation et de l'étiquetage morphosyntaxique par réseau de neurones

1.2.3 Objectif de cette contribution

Le but de cet article est d'évaluer une nouvelle fois les résultats acquis par les deux approches, celle basée sur l'utilisation des ressources du projet GREgORI (désormais GREgORI) et celle basée sur un réseau de neurones (désormais RNN, pour l'anglais *Recurrent Neural Network*).

Il faut noter que l'analyse de GREgORI ne tient pas compte du contexte et est entièrement dépendante du contenu des ressources linguistiques mises en œuvre. Cette approche fournit une ou plusieurs analyses possibles pour les mots du texte connus des ressources, mais aucun résultat pour les mots inconnus des ressources. *A contrario*, l'analyse par RNN tient compte du contexte d'apparition des mots dans le texte et propose une analyse pour tous les mots, qu'ils soient univoques, équivoques, ou inconnus du corpus d'apprentissage. Dans l'expression ի ձեռն հոգւոյն

[5] Tous les exemples arméniens cités sont tirés de l'extrait de l'*AH*.

աստուածոյ *i jern hogioyn astowacoy* « dans l'esprit de Dieu », GREgORI fournit pour la forme ի les quatre lemmes possibles hors contexte, à savoir ի *i* (la préposition), ինի *ini* (le nom de la lettre), 20 (pour le déterminant cardinal) et 20th (pour le déterminant numérique ordinal). Dans ce cas, le RNN prédit à juste titre une seule analyse : ի *i* (la préposition). En utilisant les ressources de GREgORI, l'occurrence մարդս *mards* « hommes » – attestée dans l'expression եւ զինչ մարդս բարեգործի *transcription* « traduction » –, reçoit deux analyses :

- մարդ.N+Com:Ap:Up
(une forme « simple » à l'accusatif ou au locatif pluriel)

- մարդ@u.N+Com@PRO+Dem:As:Ns:Us@Ø
(forme « composée » à l'accusatif singulier, au nominatif singulier ou au locatif singulier munie du suffixe déterminatif -u). Ici encore, le RNN prédit la forme simple, ce qui est correct.

Quand elles sont univoques, les analyses de GREgORI sont très fiables. En revanche, une révision par un expert humain reste nécessaire pour achever l'analyse des formes inconnues et ambiguës. Les analyses produites par RNN sont quant à elles des prédictions. Pour fournir un corpus parfaitement étiqueté, une révision par un expert humain est, une fois encore, indispensable. Mais l'arménien ancien reste une langue peu-dotée (Vidal-Gorène and Decours-Perez, 2020) et il semble utile de conserver les deux types d'analyse. La complémentarité des approches peut dès lors s'appréhender en considérant les dimensions de leurs zones d'ombre conjointes. Dans l'extrait de l'*AH*, GREgORI ne fournit aucune analyse pour vingt mots (soit 1,3%). Pour dix d'entre eux, RNN propose correctement le lemme et la catégorie morphosyntaxique (annexe 1, cfr 7.1). Pour six autres (soit moins de 0,4%), RNN ne propose ni le bon lemme ni la bonne catégorie morphosyntaxique (annexe 2, cfr 7.2).

Il est possible d'expliquer pourquoi GREgORI ne fournit aucune analyse pour les dix formes consignées dans l'annexe 1, cfr 7.1 :

- les trois formes զնացելում, եղելում et յաղթեցելում sont des participes post-classiques, au datif ou au locatif ;

- la présence du déterminatif -ն en finale des deux formes երեւէրն, կամէրն se justifie par le fait que ces verbes constituent les deuxièmes termes d'une proposition relative.

Ces différentes formes et différents usages ne sont pas systématiquement décrits dans les ressources du projet. Quant au verbe կացուցանեմ, il n'est tout simplement pas encore enregistré dans les lexiques de référence.

2. Évaluation

Disposant de deux approches foncièrement différentes, il est particulièrement intéressant de les confronter. L'évaluation reposera sur la comparaison des résultats de GREgORI et de RNN à ceux d'une révision manuelle (désormais Révision), car l'échantillon considéré est déjà analysé et a fait l'objet d'un premier contrôle. Dans les lignes qui suivent, nous abordons la combinatoire des situations d'accord et de désaccord entre les différentes approches et nous les illustrons d'exemples.

2.1 Accord entre GREgORI et Révision

Accord sur	Nombre	%
le lemme et la catégorie	1.505	98,37%

Tableau 5 : Accord GREgORI *vs* Révision

Dans la très grande majorité des cas, parmi les analyses fournies par GREgORI (une seule ou plusieurs) se trouve l'analyse correcte, que ce soit pour des formes simples ou composées (cfr 1.2.1).

1) այլ հաստատուն **իրաւք** ճշմարտութեան լինէր արդեւք (*AH* V 1.1), *ayl hastatun irawk' čšmartut'ean linēr ardewk'* « mais assurées par des faits véridiques »

– իրաւք,իր.N+Com:Hp –

la forme իրաւք *irawk'* « faits » a pour lemme իր *ir*, nom commun à l'instrumental pluriel.

2) եթե ոչ **վարդապետն** մեր (…) մարդ եղանիւր (*AH* V 1.1), *et'e oč' vardapetn mer (...) mard ełaniwr* « si notre maître (…) ne s'était fait homme »

– վարդապետ,.N+Com:As:Ns@ն,.PRO+Dem –

la forme վարդապետն *vardapetn* « maître » est composée de deux éléments dont les lemmes sont վարդապետ *vardapet* et -ն *-n*. Le premier est un nom commun au nominatif singulier, le second un déterminatif.

3) ո՞ այլ ոք գիտաց **զմիտս** Աստուածոյ (*AH* V 1.1) *o? ayl ok' gitac' zmits Astuacoy* « qui d'autre a connu la pensée de Dieu »

– զ,.I+Prep@միտ,.N+Com :As@ս,.PRO+Dem –

la forme զմիտս *zmits* « pensée » est composée de trois éléments dont les lemmes sont զ- *z-*, միտ *mit* et -ս *-s* qui sont respectivement une préposition, un nom commun à l'accusatif singulier et un déterminatif.

2.2 Désaccord entre GREgORI et Révision

Désaccord, GREgORI n'a	Nombre	%
aucune analyse satisfaisante (4)	25	1,63%
ou pas d'analyse (5)	20	1,31%

Tableau 6 : Désaccord GREgORI *vs* Révision

Lorsque GREgORI fournit au moins une analyse, aucune n'est correcte pour vingt-cinq mots. Enfin, GREgORI ne propose aucune analyse pour vingt mots du corpus (on a bien 98,37+1,63 = 100%). Ces deux ensembles de vingt-cinq et vingt mots n'ont, par définition, aucun mot en commun.

4) այլ **ամայի** անապատ եղելոյ (*AH* V 2.1) *ayl amayi anapat ełeloy* « mais devenu privé »

– ամայի,.A:As:Ns –

la forme ամայի *amayi* « privé » est l'adjectif ամայի au nominatif singulier. Dans les ressources de GREgORI, cette forme n'est enregistrée que sous le verbe ամամ.

5) **բարուոքն** պահեցեալ յեկեղեցւոյ (*AH* V praef.) *barwok'n pahec'eal yekełec'woy* « la [foi] bien gardée dans l'église »

– բարուոք,.A:As:Ns@ն,.PRO+Dem –

la forme բարուոքն *barwok'n* « bien » correspond à l'adjectif բարուոք *barwok'* au nominatif singulier suffixé du déterminatif -ն *-n*, lemme absent des ressources de GREgORI.

2.3 Accord entre RNN et Révision

Accord sur	Nombre	%
le lemme (6)	1201	78,50%
la catégorie (7)	1308	85,49%
le lemme et la catégorie (8)	1142	74,64%

Tableau 7 : Accord RNN *vs* Révision

6) **ամենեցուն** որք պատահիցեն գրոյս այսմիկ (*AH* V praef.) *amenec'un ork' patahic'en groys aysmik* « à tous ceux qui rencontreront ce livre »

– ամենեցուն,ամենեքեան.PRO+Ind:Âp:Dp:Gp –

la forme ամենեցուն *amenec'un* « tous » est le pronom indéfini ամենեքեան *amenek'ean* au datif pluriel. RNN a bien prédit le lemme mais le caractérise comme nom commun.

7) ո՞ այլ ոք խորհրդակից եղեւ **նորա** (*AH* V 1.1) *o? ayl ok' xorhrdakic' ełew nora* « qui d'autre a été son conseiller ? »

– նորա, նա (նա).PRO+Dem:Gs –

la forme նորա est le génitif singulier du pronom démonstratif նա dont le lemme est նա (նա) afin d'éviter l'homographie avec la conjonction նա (եւ). La forme est fréquente. Pourtant, RNN propose un lemme նա (սա), sans doute présent, erronément, dans le corpus d'apprentissage.

8) ոչ **բռնադատելով** առնուլ զորս կամէրն (*AH* V 1.1) *oč' bṙnadatelov aṙnul zors kamērn* « ne forçant pas à prendre celles qu'il voulait »

– բռնադատելով,բռնադատեմ.V:KHs:WHs –

RNN propose pour la forme բռնադատելով *bṙnadatelov* « forçant », du lemme verbal բռնադատեմ *bṙnadatem*, au participe et à l'instrumental singulier.

2.4 Désaccord entre RNN et Révision

Désaccord sur	Nombre	%
la catégorie, mais accord sur le lemme (9)	59	3,86%
le lemme, mais accord sur la catégorie (10)	166	10,85%
le lemme et la catégorie (11, 12)	163	10,65%

Tableau 8 : Désaccord RNN *vs* Révision

9) **որպէս** երանելի առաքեալն ասէ (*AH* V 2.3) *orpēs eraneli aṙak'ealn asē* « comme le bienheureux apôtre dit »

– որպէս,.I+Conj –

La conjonction որպէս *orpēs* est erronément caractérisé comme un adverbe par RNN, analyse sans doute présente, erronément, dans le corpus d'apprentissage.

10) եւ յայլ եւս ի մարդն **գոյացութենէ** (*AH* V 2.2) *ew yayl ews i mardn goyac'ut'enē* « et du reste de la substance de l'homme »

– գոյացութենէ,գոյացութիւն.N+Com:Âs –

la forme գոյացութենէ *goyac'ut'enē* « substance » doit être comprise comme l'ablatif singulier du nom commun գոյացութիւն *goyac'ut'iwn*. RNN propose un nom commun, mais lui attribue un lemme qui n'existe pas : գոյանութիւն.

11) ի **լաւէն** զառ նա (*AH* V 1.1) *i lawēn zaṙ na* « à partir du bon auprès de lui »

– լաւէ,լաւ,A:Âs@ն,.PRO+Dem –

la forme լաւէն *lawēn* est l'ablatif singulier de l'adjectif լաւ accompagnée du suffixe déterminatif -ն. RNN suggère une analyse possible, à savoir une forme conjuguée du verbe լսեմ. Mais cette prédiction ne convient pas *in textu.*

12) որ (…) ի **հացէ** որ մարմին նորա աճէր (*AH* V 2.2) *or (…) i hac'ē or marmin nora ačēr* « qui (…) s'accroissait par le pain qui est son corps »

– հացէ,հաց.N+Com:Âs –

la forme հացէ est l'ablatif singulier du nom commun հաց *hac'* « pain ». RNN prédit un lemme verbal հաց. Le RNN prédit trente-six lemmes verbaux impropres car ne se terminant pas par -ամ, -եմ, -իմ ou -ում.

2.5 Accord entre GREgORI et RNN

Après avoir aborder chaque outil isolément, nous prenons ici en compte leur accord sur une même analyse. Dans 73,86% des cas la prédiction du RNN correspond à une des analyses possibles proposées par GREgORI. C'est accord peut être correct ou fautif.

Accord sur	Nombre	%
le lemme et la catégorie qui sont corrects (13)	1.130	73,86%

Tableau 9 : Accord GREgORI, RNN *vs* Révision

13) զի եւ զէնթադրութիւնս զայս **գիտասցես** (*AH* V praef.) *zi ew zent'adrut'iwns zays gitasc'es* « afin que tu connaisses aussi ses arguments »

– գիտասցես,գիտեմ.V:ESJ2s –

les deux outils classent la forme գիտասցես sous le lemme verbal գիտեմ.

Dans l'exemple qui suit, les deux outils s'accordent cependant sur une analyse erronée. Cela peut s'expliquer par le fait que RNN a été entraîné sur les données de GRE*g*ORI dans lesquelles cette analyse fautive est présente.

14) Եւ եթէ ոչ **ապրեսցի** սա (*AH* V 2.2) *Ew et'e oč' apresc'i sa* « et si elle n'était pas sauvée »

– ապրեսցի,ապրիմ.V:MSJ3s –

Les deux outils s'accordent bien sur la nature verbale du mot, mais propose un lemme actif ապրեմ au lieu de ապրիմ (« se sauver »).

3. Conclusions et perspectives

Les données de GRE*g*ORI et de la Révision s'accordent dans 98,37% des cas (cfr 2.1). Cela plaide en faveur de l'analyse produite par GRE*g*ORI. Les données de RNN et de la Révision (cfr 2.3) s'accordent dans 74,64% des cas. L'accord entre GRE*g*ORI et RNN concerne 73,86% des cas (cfr 2.5). Ces deux derniers résultats sont donc inférieurs au premier. En revanche, quand, à vingt reprises, GRE*g*ORI ne fournit aucune analyse, RNN prédit dix analyses correctes, tant au niveau du lemme que de la catégorie morphosyntaxique (cfr 1.2.3). Ces résultats sont illustrés dans la figure 1 (voir aussi l'annexe 1, cfr 7.1).

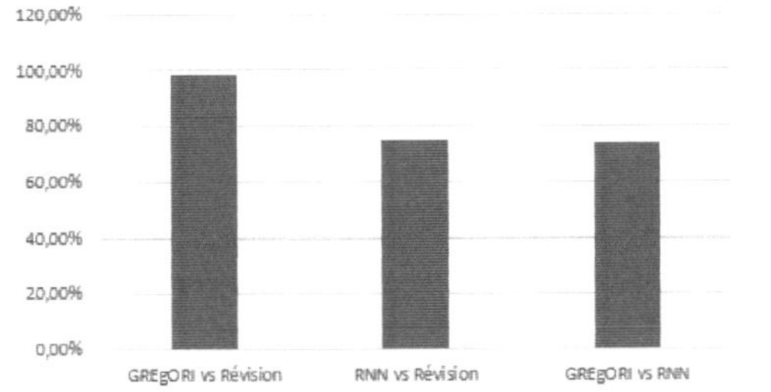

Figure 1 : Accords sur les lemmes et les catégories morphosyntaxiques

Lorsqu'elles ne s'accordent pas, ces deux approches demeurent complémentaires. Les cas où elles n'ont ni l'une ni l'autre la bonne analyse restent minoritaires : GRE*g*ORI *vs* Révision, 1,63% (cfr 2.2), RNN *vs* Révision, 10,65% (cfr 2.4). Ces données sont illustrées dans la figure 2. Par ailleurs, aucun outil n'invalide l'autre et leur utilisation conjointe permet même au réviseur humain de travailler efficacement. Quand, à vingt reprises, GRE*g*ORI ne fournit aucune analyse, RNN se trompe six fois sur le lemme et sur la catégorie morphosyntaxique (voir aussi l'annexe 2, cfr 7.2). Les autres résultats sont corrects.

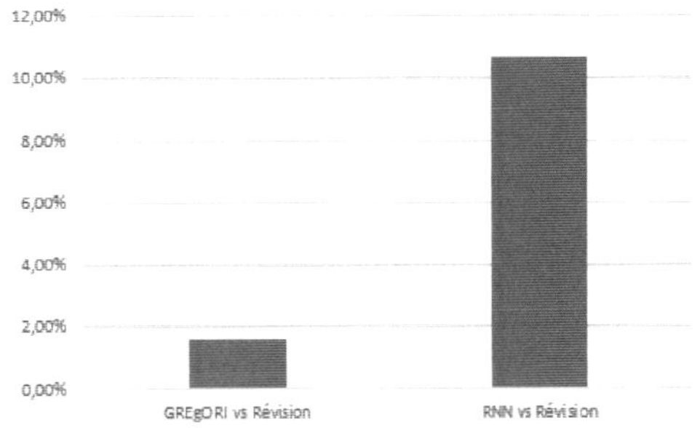

Figure 2 : Désaccords sur les lemmes et sur les catégories morphosyntaxiques

Les corrections apportées lors de la révision manuelle enrichissent les données. Pour les ressources de GRE*g*ORI, ce sont des ajouts de formes nouvelles, simples ou composées, ou de lemmes inédits, incluant les informations morphosynatxiques et flexionnelles correspondant aux formes concernées. Il y a aussi des corrections. Pour RNN, les données lemmatisées de chaque nouveau texte traité rejoignent, après révision, le corpus d'apprentissage utilisé pour construire, tester et évaluer le réseau de neurones, avant son utilisation sur de nouveaux textes (cfr 1.2.2).

Plus ces outils seront utilisés, meilleurs ils seront. Le projet GRE*g*ORI est basé sur les itérations successives de ses outils et sur leur hybridation. Plusieurs corpus sont actuellement en cours de traitement ou de révision. L'examen des analyses produites ou prédites à l'occasion du traitement de ces textes permettra d'objectiver l'évolution progressive des performances de ces deux approches et de les comparer aux résultats acquis précédemment. À court ou moyen termes, l'accroissement des données déjà analysées permettra de paramétrer le RNN pour qu'il prédise aussi les analyses flexionnelles.

Après les inévitables phases de développement, d'implémentation et de test (comme décrit dans Vidal-Gorène and Kindt, 2020 ; Vidal-Gorène and Kindt, 2022 ; Kindt, Vidal-Gorène et Delle Donne, 2022), l'approche hybride combinant les analyses « par dictionnaire » et par « réseau de neurones » entre dans une phase de réelle production, en arménien, mais aussi dans les autres langues de l'Orient chrétien (géorgien, syriaque,grec, etc.). Outre le livre V de l'*AH* d'Irénée, en cours de traitement sous la responsabilité de Gabriel Kepeklian (cfr 1.1 et note 1), les textes arméniens de deux volumes du CSCO ont ou vont bientôt rejoindre les données lemmatisées de GRE*g*ORI. Bernard Coulie a analysé le *Commentaire à la Genèse* attribué à Step'anos de Siwnik' (CSCO 695, Scrip. Arm. 32) publié par M.E. Stone, ainsi que la version arménienne des *Lettres* d'Évagre le Pontique (CSCO 704, Scrip. Arm. 33) publiée par R. Darling Young et H. Karapetyan. Par ailleurs, l'analyse de tous les volumes arméniens du CSCO est en cours, en collaboration avec Peeters Publishers. Emmanuel Van Elverdinghe assure l'analyse des trois versions arméniennes déjà éditées le l'*Apocalypse* de Jean, (Murat, 1905 ; Conybeare, 1907 ; Zōhrapean, 1805), ainsi que celle des textes des Colophons des manuscrits arméniens (Van

Elverdinghe, 2018 ; Van Elverdinghe, 2022 ; Van Elverdinghe et Kindt, 2022).

4. Remerciements

Les auteurs tiennent à exprimer leur gratitude envers le Professeur Bernard Coulie (UCLouvain), Chahan Vidal-Gorène (Calfa), et Emmanuel Van Elverdinghe (UCLouvain).

5. Bibliographical References

Conybeare, F.C. (1907). The Armenian Version of Revelation and Cyril of Alexandria's Scholia on the Incarnation and Epistle on Easter. *Text and Translation Society*, 5. London : p. 1-32.

Coulie, B., Kindt, B., Kepeklian, G. & Van Elverdinghe, E. (2022). Étiquettes morphosyntaxiques et flexionnelles pour le traitement automatique de l'arménien ancien. *Le Muséon*, 135 (1-2): p. 209-241.

Kepeklian, G. (2021). La version arménienne du Livre V de l'*Adversus haereses* d'Irénée de Lyon : histoire du texte, édition critique, traduction et notes (Thèse de doctorat), UCLouvain, Louvain-la-Neuve.

Kindt, B., Vidal-Gorène, Ch. & Delle Donne, S. (2022). Analyse automatique du grec ancien par réseau de neurones. Évaluation sur le corpus *De Thessalonica Capta*. *BABELAO*, 10-11: p. 537-562.

Murat, Fr. (1905-1911). Յայտնութեանն Յովհաննու հին հայ թարգմանութիւն *(Yaytnut'eann Yovhannu hin hay t'argmanut'iwn) / Die Offenbarung Johannis in einer alten armenischen Übersetzung*). Jerusalem: p. 3-76.

Rousseau, A. (1984), Irénée de Lyon, Contre les hérésies. Dénonciation et réfutation de la gnose au nom menteur (Sagesses Chrétiennes). Paris: Les éditions du Cerf.

Van Elverdinghe, E. & Kindt, B. (2022). Describing Language Variation in the Colophons of Armenian Manuscripts. LREC 2022. Submitted.

Van Elverdinghe, E. (2018). Recurrent Pattern Modelling in a Corpus of Armenian Manuscript Colophons. Journal of Data Mining and Digital Humanities, Special Issue on Computer-Aided Processing of Intertextuality in Ancient Languages.

Van Elverdinghe, E. (2022). Modèles et copies. Étude d'une formule des colophons de manuscrits arméniens (VIIIe-XIXe siècles). Louvain: Peeters.

Vidal-Gorène, Ch. & Decours-Perez, A. (2020). Languages Resources for Poorly Endowed Languages: The Case Study of Classical Armenian. In N. Calzolari *et al.* (Eds.), *LREC 2020, Marseille. Twelfth International Conference on Language Resources and Evaluation, May 11-16, 2020, Palais du Pharo, Marseille, France: Conference proceedings*, p. 3145-3152). Paris: The European Language Resources Association (ELRA).

Vidal-Gorène, Ch. & Kindt, B. (2020). Lemmatization and POS-tagging process by using joint learning approach. Experimental results on Classical Armenian, Old Georgian, and Syriac. In R. Sprugnoli & M. Passarotti (Eds.), *1st Workshop on Language Technologies for Historical and Ancient Languages, (LT4HALA 2020): Proceedings*, p. 22-27. Paris: European Language Resources Association (ELRA).

Vidal-Gorène, Ch. & Kindt, B. (2022). From manuscript to tagged corpora. An automated process for Ancient Armenian or other under resourced languages of the Christian East. *Armeniaca*, 1. Submitted.

Zōhrapean, Y. (1805). Ա(ստուա)ծաշունչ մատեան հին եւ նոր կտակարանաց (*Astuacašunč' matean hin ew nor ktakaranac' / God-Breathed Scriptures of the Old and New Testaments*), Venice : p. 825-836.

6. Language Resource References

Calfa. (depuis 2014). Calfa, https://calfa.fr.

GREgORI Project. (since 1990). GREgORI – Software, linguistic data and tagged corpora for ancient GREek and ORIental languages, https://uclouvain.be/fr/instituts-recherche/incal/ciol/gregori-project.html, ISSN 2736-7657.

7. Annexes

7.1 Annexe 1 : Liste des formes inconnues de GRE*g*ORI mais analysées correctement par RNN

Forme (token)	Lemme	Catégorie morphosyntaxique
գնացելում	գնամ	V
եղելում	եղանիմ	V
զաստուածոյն	զ@աստուած	I+Prep@N+Com@PRO+Dem
կամէրն	կամիմ@ն	V@PRO+Dem
երեւէրն	երեւիմ@ն	V@PRO+Dem
երեւէրն	երեւիմ@ն	V@PRO+Dem
յաղթեցելում	յաղթեմ	V
կացուցէ	կացուցանեմ	V
զվերստին	զ@վերստին	I+Prep@I+Adv
զանդրէն	զ@անդրէն	I+Prep@I+Adv

Cfr explication en 1.2.3.

7.2 Annexe 2 : Liste des formes inconnues de GRE*g*ORI et analysées erronément par RNN

Forme (token)	RNN		Révision	
	Lemme	Catégorie morphosyntaxique	Lemme	Catégorie morphosyntaxique
կատարելոյն	կատարելի	A	կատարելի@ն	A@PRO+Dem
այժմս	այժմ	I+Adv	այժմ@ս	I+Adv@PRO+Dem
բարուոքն	բարուոք@ն	NUM+Ord	բարի@ն	A@PRO+Dem
բարձրելոյն	բարձրեալ	A	բարձրանամ	V
շարունակէն	շարունական	A	շարունակեմ@ն	V@PRO+Dem
բարձրելոյն	բարձրեալ	A	բարձրանամ@ն	V@PRO+Dem

Cfr explication en 2.4.

7.3 Annexe 3 : Liste des étiquettes morphosyntaxiques (POS) (tiré de Coulie, Kindt, Kepeklian et Van Elverdinghe, 2022)

Étiquette	Description	Étiquette	Description
A	Adjectif	NUM+Car	Déterminant numérique cardinal (mot)
I+Adv	Mot invariable – Adverbe	NUM+Ord	Déterminant numérique ordinal (mot)
I+AdvPr	Mot invariable – Adverbe prépositionnel	NUMA+Car	Déterminant numérique cardinal (lettre)
I+Conj	Mot invariable – Conjonction	NUMA+Ord	Déterminant numérique ordinal (lettre)
I+Intj	Mot invariable – Interjection	PRO+Dem	Pronom démonstratif
I+Neg	Mot invariable – Négation	PRO+Ind	Pronom indéfini
I+Part	Mot invariable – Particule	PRO+Int	Pronom interrogatif
I+Prep	Mot invariable – Préposition	PRO+Per[1,2][s,p]	Pronom personnel
N+Ant	Nom propre anthroponymique	PRO+Pos[1,2][s,p]	Pronom possessif
N+Com	Nom commun	PRO+Rec	Pronom réciproque
N+Let	Nom d'une lettre	PRO+Ref	Pronom réfléchi
N+Pat	Nom propre patronymique	PRO+Rel	Pronom relatif
N+Prop	Nom propre	V	Verbe
N+Top	Nom propre toponymique		

7.4 **Annexe 4 : Liste des étiquettes flexionnelles** (tiré de Coulie, Kindt, Kepeklian et Van Elverdinghe, 2022)

Type d'étiquette	Étiquette	Description	Type d'étiquette	Étiquette	Description
Cas	N	Nominatif	Mode	Î	Indicatif
	A	Accusatif		K	Participe
	G	Génitif		S	Subjonctif
	D	Datif		Y	Impératif
	U	Locatif		W	Infinitif
	Â	Ablatif	Temps	P	Présent
	H	Instrumental		I	Imparfait
Nombre	s	Singulier		J	Aoriste
	p	Pluriel	Personne	1	Première personne
Voix	E	Actif		2	Deuxième personne
	B	Passif		3	Troisième personne
	M	Moyen-passif			

Proceedings of the Workshop on Processing Language Variation: Digital Armenian (DigitAm 2022) @LREC2022, pages 21–27
Marseille, 20 June 2022

Describing Language Variation in the Colophons of Armenian Manuscripts

Emmanuel Van Elverdinghe, Bastien Kindt
Centre d'études orientales – Institut orientaliste de Louvain (CIOL),
Institut des civilisations, arts et lettres (INCAL),
UCLouvain, Louvain-la-Neuve, Belgium
{emmanuel.vanelverdinghe,bastien.kindt}@uclouvain.be

Abstract

The colophons of Armenian manuscripts constitute a large textual corpus spanning a millennium of written culture. These texts are highly diverse and rich in terms of linguistic variation. This poses a challenge to NLP tools, especially considering the fact that linguistic resources designed or suited for Armenian are still scarce. In this paper, we deal with a sub-corpus of colophons written to commemorate the rescue of a manuscript and dating from 1286 to ca. 1450, a thematic group distinguished by a particularly high concentration of words exhibiting linguistic variation. The text is processed (lemmatization, POS-tagging, and inflectional tagging) using the tools of the GREgORI Project and evaluated. Through a selection of examples, we show how variation is dealt with at each linguistic level (phonology, orthography, flexion, vocabulary, syntax). Complex variation, at the level of tokens or lemmata, is considered as well. The results of this work are used to enrich and refine the linguistic resources of the GREgORI project, which in turn benefits the processing of other texts.

Keywords: Ancient Armenian, colophons, lemmatization, POS-tagging, inflectional tagging, language variation

1. Preliminary notes and aims

1.1 The colophons of Armenian manuscripts

In the traditional sense, a colophon is a record of completion of a book by its scribe. The Armenian concept of *yišatakaran* (literally "memorial", usually translated as colophon), has a broader meaning, encompassing practically all significant annotations in manuscripts besides scholia or glosses, including personal notes left by later owners or readers. Colophons are an important part of the Armenian literary culture, where they are recognized as a full-fledged genre. As a result, they have attracted the interest of scholars for a long time, but especially since 1950, when the first systematic collection of colophons appeared in print. Since then, most colophons written until 1500 have been published in these dedicated collections, as well as colophons from the period 1601–1660.

This paper deals with a particular sub-corpus of non-scribal colophons recording the rescue of a manuscript, usually from the hands of Muslim captors. Using the abovementioned printed collections (Xačʻikyan, 1955, 1967, 1950; Xačʻikyan, Matʻevosyan, and Łazarosyan, 2018, 2020; Matʻevosyan, 1984), we identified 46 such colophons in the period leading up to 1450. The earliest of them was written in 1286; however, in several cases, the exact date is unknown and an approximate dating has been inferred. The text of these colophons was extracted from the corpus of Armenian colophons maintained at the UCLouvain and lemmatized according to the principles of the GREgORI Project (Coulie, Kindt, Kepeklian, and Van Elverdinghe, 2022). The main corpus of Armenian colophons currently comprises 1.232.652 tokens (Table 1, section A).

1.2 Language variation in Armenian

Variation affects all areas of language, occurring at the phonetical, morphological, lexical, syntactic, semantic, and pragmatic levels, and is mainly expressed across four dimensions: diachronic, diatopic, diastratic, and diaphasic (Auer and Schmidt, 2010: 226–228). This contribution focuses on phonetical, morphological, and lexical variation in Armenian colophons within the diachronic, diatopic, and diaphasic dimensions. Proper names (anthroponyms and toponyms) are not considered here: the problems posed by this very abundant and versatile category ought to be considered separately. Upon manual inspection, the sub-corpus was found to contain an estimated 473 anthroponyms, 7 patronymics, and 82 toponyms, adding up to a provisional total of 562 tokens, or 9.62% of all tokens in the sub-corpus (see Table 1). This percentage is almost doubled if one considers unique tokens instead of all tokens (18.30%).

	Tokens	Unique tokens
Anthroponyms (N+Ant)	473	345
Patronymics (N+Pat)	7	7
Toponyms (N+Top)	82	71
Proper nouns total	562	421
As percentage of sub-corpus	9.62%	18.30%

Table 1: Quantitative assessment (estimation) of proper nouns in the sub-corpus

The high variability and unpredictability of these categories creates a serious challenge. As an example, the only attestation of the name Երեւան *Erewan* in the sub-corpus, does not refer to the current capital of Armenia, but to an elderly priest. But the main difficulty with processing a proper noun lies in formulating an adequate lemma, owing to the number of different variants, spellings, and paradigms attested in the texts. For instance, the name George appears variously in the sub-corpus as Գէորգ *Gēorg*, Գէորգէոս *Gēorgēos*, and Գորգ *Gorg*. In addition to such true variants, there is the widespread issue of scribal inconsistency, which cannot always be easily resolved. In the following case, one colophon has as many as four different spellings for the same toponym: Սիւնայվանից *Siwnayvanicʻ*, Սիւնեվանից *Siwnevanicʻ*, Սիւնէվանից *Siwnēvanicʻ*,

and Սիւնիվանք *Siwnivank'*. These questions, however interesting, outstretch the aims of the present paper and should be dealt with at a later stage.
Specific studies have been devoted to various aspects of linguistic variation in Armenian colophons, focusing principally on the period from the 12th to the 15th century: sound change (Harut'yunyan, 2014b), diachronic morphology (Harut'yunyan, 2014a; Hovsep'yan, 1997), dialectal features (J̌ahukyan, 1997), neologisms (Margaryan, 1993), anthroponymy (Harut'yunyan, 2018a, 2018b; Weitenberg, 2005), and stylistic patterns (Van Elverdinghe, 2018, 2022). Obviously, these developments of the Middle Armenian idiom are not specific to colophons. Most of them have been described by (Karst, 1901), drawing from literary, legal, medical, etc., texts. Since then, numerous studies have enriched our knowledge of Middle Armenian. (Weitenberg, 1995), dealing with poetical texts, set a blueprint for the investigation of linguistic variation in Middle Armenian sources.
The sub-corpus studied here was selected because it shows a more diverse linguistic picture than a random sampling of Armenian colophons of the same period would. This is due to the fact that many colophons of this group are not written by professional scribes and do not follow the customs and patterns of colophon writing. Therefore, the widespread tendency to normalization and conformity to the rules of Classical Armenian recedes, while the spoken Middle Armenian idiom infiltrates the written medium. This allows for more or less considerable linguistic variation within each colophon.

1.3 Linguistic resources of the GRE*g*ORI Project

The automated analysis of this sub-corpus of Armenian colophons was carried out using tools and linguistic data of the (GRE*g*ORI Project). The Armenian language shares characteristics of both inflectional and agglutinative languages. As such, inflected simple forms can receive prepositional suffixes as well as determinative suffixes. In their current state, the linguistic resources of the GRE*g*ORI Project consist of a set of 315.952 simple word-forms (i.e. inflected words such as աշխատողաց *ašxatołac'*), on the one hand, and a set of 883.171 polylexical forms (such as զաշխատողացն, i.e. զ-աշխատողաց-ն *z-ašxatołac'-n*), on the other hand. Together, these two sets totalize 1.199.123 tokens, simple or polylexical, which are recorded along with 30.311 lemmata (lexical entries) and the corresponding part-of-speech of these lemmata. Word-forms are either taken from the corpora already processed in the past or generated automatically (under human supervision) in order to improve, as much as possible, the lexical coverage during the processing of new corpora. The sum of these data constitutes a reference lexicon (Coulie, Kindt, Kepeklian, and Van Elverdinghe, 2022). On that basis, the main goals of the GRE*g*ORI Project can be reached, viz to provide scholars with tagged corpora, lemmatized concordances or indexes, and online, searchable corpora.

2. Processing and preliminary evaluation

The processing phase consists in lemmatization, POS-tagging, and inflectional tagging. It is subdivided in three steps, as described in (Kindt, Vidal-Gorène, and Delle Donne, 2022; Vidal-Gorène and Kindt, 2022): 1) analysis by lexical look-up, matching the vocabulary of the corpus with the data gathered in the reference lexicon; 2) analysis using an RNN model; 3) manual check of the analysed data. Only then can scholars be provided with a final, tagged corpus. The first step ensures a highly accurate tagging, but fails to identify unknown words and does not solve lexical ambiguities. The second step resorts to an RNN model previously trained with already processed corpora of the GRE*g*ORI Project and applied by Calfa to the study of new corpora. In that case, the outcomes are complete, since the process does not disregard unknown words and resolves lexical ambiguity. However, they remain statistical predictions, and not analyses grounded on a common linguistic approach. A considerable advantage to this hybrid approach is that it alleviates the human intervention necessary during the third step, before the final data can be delivered (Kindt, Vidal-Gorène, and Delle Donne, 2022; Vidal-Gorène and Kindt, 2020).
A PDF version of the lemmatized concordance of the sub-corpus is available on the GRE*g*ORI website[1]. The sub-corpus is also available on the online interfaces of the GRE*g*ORI Project[2].

Section A – Main corpus of Armenian colophons	
Tokens	1.232.652
Unique tokens	144.347
Section B – Sub-corpus of Armenian colophons	
Tokens	5.845
Unique tokens	2.300
Step 1 – Analysis by lexical look-up	
Lemma = 0	1.263
Lemma = 1	3.281
Lemmata > 1	1.301
Step 2 – Analysis using an RNN model	
Lemma = 1	5.845
Step 3 – Checking results (April 2022)	
Already checked	4.381

Table 2: Number of tokens and unique tokens in the Armenian colophons (main corpus and sub-corpus)

Table 2 presents (section A) the number of tokens and unique tokens in the main corpus of Armenian colophons, and (section B) the number of of tokens and unique tokens in the sub-corpus of colophons studied in this paper, along with (*step 1*) quantitative results obtained after the first step of the analysis (number of

[1] https://uclouvain.be/fr/instituts-recherche/incal/ciol/gregori-project.html

[2] https://www.gregoriproject.com

tokens without lemma, with one lemma, with more than one lemma). For the reasons explained above, the results obtained by RNN (*step 2*) are equal to the total number of words. Finally (*step 3*), the current number of already checked results is given.
The lexical analysis of Armenian colophons (main corpus or sub-corpus) is still a work in progress. Most notably, the analysis and lemmatization of proper nouns has been deferred to a later date (see above, 1.2). Nonetheless, the current results already allow using lemmata, POS-tags and inflectional analysis to explore adequately the sub-corpus under consideration. Indeed, tagged data are very helpful in order to describe language variation in the sub-corpus and to single out relevant examples. Many of the 1.263 unknown words (Lemma = 0) highlighted during step 1 (see table 2) are examples of linguistic variation: they bear witness to non-classical strata of the Armenian language that are not yet fully described in the linguistic resources of the GREgORI Project.

3. Selected examples of linguistic variation

The following examples are organized according to the linguistic level at which they occur. They are meant as a representative sample of the different phenomena attested in the corpus, and of their description in the linguistic resources of the GREgORI Project. The issue of which dialect, period, etc., is affected by these variations is too complex to be dealt with here. The same goes for the precise linguistic constraints surrounding these changes[3]. All these examples concern words for which the resources of the GREgORI Project fail to offer an analysis, counted in the 1.263 unknown words ("lemma = 0") quoted in table 1 (*step 1*).

3.1 Phonology

At the phoneme level, the language of colophons reflects the general evolution of the Armenian vocalic system, including monophthongization and merger of some sounds (except at the beginning of words), such as: *aw* (also written *ō*) > *o* (1), *ē* > *e*, *ea(y)* > *ē* (= *e*) (2). Consonants are subject to multiple variations, among which one can cite, in addition to the well-known consonant shift affecting a number of dialects, the devoicing and aspiration of voiced consonants in certain contexts (3), and the devoicing of final deictic *-d* (4).

1) H14 681, p. 546 l. 6: *šošap'-oł-ac'* (touch-AGN-GEN/DAT/ABL.PL) "handlers" (Cl. շաւշափողաց *šawšap'ołac'*)
= շոշափողաց,շաւշափող.N+Com:ÂpDpGp
2) H15A 699, p. 619 l. 37: ցորէն *c'orēn* "wheat" (Cl. ցորեան *c'orean*)
= ցորէն,ցորեան.N+Com:AsNsUs
3) H14 685, p. 549 l. 20: աւագ *awak'* "greater, senior" (Cl. աւագ *awag*)
= աւաք,աւագ.A
4) H15A 616, p. 543 l. 6: աղաւթքտ *aławt'-k'-t* (prayer-NOM.PL-that) "your prayers" (Cl. աղաւթքդ *aławt'k'd*)
= աղաւթք,աղաւթք.N+Com:Np@տ,դ.PRO+Dem

3.2 Orthography

These sound changes in turn gave rise to incorrect or hypercorrect spellings. For instance, the medieval letter *ō*, which stands for the old diphthong *aw* in positions where the latter was monophthongized, is also incorrectly used where *aw* was actually realized as /av/ (5). Another orthographical feature is that the epenthetic schwa is occasionally written in positions where, according to the spelling rules of Classical Armenian, it should not appear (6).

5) H14 685, p. 549 l. 19: օետարանս *ōetaran-s* (gospel-this) "this Gospel [book]" (Cl. աւետարանս *awetarans*)
= օետարան,աւետարան.N+Com:AsNs@ս,ս.PRO+Dem
6) H14B 799, p. 447 l. 10: վերըստին *verəstin* "once again" (Cl. վերստին *verstin*)
= վերըստին,վերստին.I+Adv

3.3 Declension

A number of words undergo paradigmatic reorganization, changing from one thematic paradigm to another (7) or, in the case of irregular paradigms, switching to a regular, thematic paradigm (8; 9). In parallel, several new endings develop, notably plurals in *-(n)er* (10) and locatives in *-um* (11).

7) H15A 129, p. 128 l. 38: սպասիւք *spas-iwk'* (service-INSTR.PL) "with [liturgical] vessels" (Cl. սպասուք *spasuk'*)
= սպասիւք,սպաս.N+Com:Hp
8) H13 478b, p. 595 l. 12: փոքրի *p'ok'r-i* (small-GEN/DAT/LOC.SG) "small" (Cl. փոքու *p'ok'u*)
= փոքրի,փոքր.A:DsGsUs
9) H15A 38, p. 40 l. 34: զվաներն *z-van-er-n* (DOBJ-monastery-PL-the) "the monasteries" (Cl. զվանսն *zvansn*)
= զ,զ.I+Prep@վաներ,վանք.N+Com:Ap:Np:Up@ն,ն.PRO+Dem
10) H15C 544, p. 403 l. 28: քուվերաց *k'uver-ac'* (sister-GEN/DAT/ABL.PL) "sisters" (Cl. քերց *k'erc'*)
= քուվերաց,քոյր.N+Com:ÂpDpGp
11) H14 676, p. 543 l. 19: ի հանդերձելումն *i handerj-el-um-n* (in prepare-PART-LOC-the) "in the future"
= ի,ի.I+Prep
հանդերձելում,հանդերձեմ.V:KUs@
ն,ն.PRO+Dem

3.4 Conjugation

Similar evolutions characterize the verbal system. Monosyllabic third person singular aorist forms receive an augment in *e-* or *ē-* (12), or *er-* if they already

[3] For further information about these linguistic phenomena, the reader is referred to the works cited above (1.2).

had an augment in Classical Armenian. The latter evolution applies, among others, to verb *tam* "to give", which even gets a whole new aorist paradigm (13). An important element in the reconfiguration of the verbal system is the emergence of a particle *ku* (*kə* / *k-*) to mark the indicative mood (14).

12) H14 679a, p. 544 l. 35: էզարկ *ē-zark* (AOR.3.SG-strike) "[the khan] struck" (Cl. զարկ *zark*)
= էզարկ,զարկանեմ.V:EÎJ3s
13) H15A 418b, p. 392 l. 21: տուի *tu-i* (give-AOR.1.SG) "I gave"
= տուի,տամ.V:EÎJ1s (Cl. ետու *etu*)
14) H14B 670, p. 295 l. 32: կուզէր *k-uz-ēr* (IND-want-IMPFT.3.SG) "[the sultan] wanted"
= կ,կու (կը).I+Part@ուզէր,ուզեմ.V:EÎI3s

3.5 Vocabulary

The vocabulary of colophons includes words not found in classical texts, such as dialectal or colloquial words (15), neologisms (16), and loan-words (17; 18). Purely semantic variations are, as a rule, not recorded by the GREgORI project.

15) H14B 670, p. 295 l. 6: յիշուեց *yišu-ec'* (plunder-AOR.3.SG) "he plundered"
= յիշուեց,յիշվեմ.V:EÎJ3s
16) H15A 1*, p. 3 n. 1 l. 5: նեղաչուի *nełač'ui* "slant-eyed", from նեղ *neł* "narrow" and աչուի *ač'ui* (Cl. աչք *ač'k'*) "eyes"
= նեղաչուի.A
17) H14 593d, p. 484 l. 32: հալալ *halal* "legitimate", from Arabic حَلَال *ḥalāl*
= հալալ.A
18) H14 681, p. 546 l. 16: պարոն *paron* "sir", from French *baron*
= պարոն.N+Com

3.6 Syntax

The syntax of colophons shows a number of peculiarities, some of which are common to other Middle Armenian literary texts. As an example, one can cite the fact that the nominative plural ending *-k'* is increasingly used for the direct object, instead of the accusative plural ending *-s* (especially with *pluralia tantum*) (19).

19) H14B 670, p. 296 l. 1: կատարեաց զսուլտանին կամքն *katar-eac' z-sultan-i-n kam-k'-n* "he fulfilled the sultan's wish" (fulfil-AOR.3.SG DOBJ-sultan-GEN.SG-the will-NOM.PL-the)
= կատարեաց,կատարեմ.V:EÎJ3s
զ,զ.I+Prep@
սուլտանի,սուլտան.N+Com@ն,ն.PRO+Dem
կամք,կամ (կամաց).N+Com:Np@ն,ն.PRO+Dem

4. Complex variation

In some of the examples given above, more than one feature can be ascribed to linguistic variation. Thus in (14), not only is the particle կ- *k-* an innovation, but the verbal lemma itself, ուզեմ *uzem* "to want", is a Middle Armenian variant of the classical verb յուզեմ *yuzem* "to seek", in which a sound change (loss of the initial glide) coincides with semantic evolution.

Likewise, some lemmata concentrate different instances of variation, as lemmatized concordances readily show. Appendix 9.1 lists the attested tokens of the lemma բերդ *berd*, one of three words with the meaning of "fortress, castle" in the sub-corpus (the other two being ամրոց *amroc'* and կլա *kla*). The words բերդերն *berdern*, բերդերոյն *berderoyn*, բերդերովն *berderovn*, and զբերդերն *zberdern* illustrate the plural formation in *-(n)er* (9)—notice how not a single classical plural form of this lemma is found in the sub-corpus—, while բե[ր]թի *be[r]t'i* is a case of devoicing and aspiration of a voiced consonant after *r* (3).

Appendix 9.2 presents a concordance of the lemma տամ *tam* "to give", showing several non-classical forms of the active aorist paradigm (13): first person singular տուի *tui*, third person singular երետ *eret* and էրետ *ēret* (12), and first person plural տըւինք *təwink'* (6) and տւինք *twink'*. In addition, the sub-corpus contains an occurrence of the Middle Armenian participial form տված *tvac*, appearing as part of a periphrastic past tense.

5. Conclusion

The corpus of Armenian colophons constitutes an invaluable collection of texts, both historically and linguistically (Harut'yunyan, 2019; Stone, 1995; etc.). The language of this corpus stands out for its diachronic, diatopic, and diaphasic variation. Therefore, a systematic analysis of the vocabulary of colophons using NLP tools will be helpful to increase our knowledge and understanding of the varieties, evolution, and uses of the Armenian language.

The resources of the GREgORI Project have already facilitated an investigation into the formulaic patterns that characterize the style of Armenian colophons (Van Elverdinghe, 2018, 2022). Lemmatization, POS-tagging, and inflectional tagging of the corpus make it possible to successfully execute complex search queries, such as is required to detect and analyse speech patterns.

The long-term goal is to achieve full lemmatization of the whole corpus of Armenian colophons; in the meantime, applications on more limited sub-corpora like the one under consideration here are expected. Enriching the linguistic resources of the GREgORI Project with forms found in colophons also represents a step forward towards the treatment of other Middle Armenian texts, especially texts of a documentary nature, such as inscriptions, of which there is already an example on the GREgORI website (Goepp, Mutafian, & Ouzounian, 2012).

As regards the processing of proper nouns, two avenues could be explored. One relies on manual lemmatization of newly-encountered forms, basing the decisions on reference works such as (Ačaṙyan, 1942–1962) for anthroponyms and (Hakobyan, Melik'-Bašxyan, and Barsełyan 1986–2001) for toponyms. The other path entails complete or partial automation of the initial process using an existing dataset. Unfortunately, any corpus designed for modern Eastern Armenian, such as (pioNER, 2018—see Ghukasyan *et al.*, 2018), can hardly be exploited from a Classical or Middle Armenian perspective. The most appealing prospect at this point is the ongoing digitization and full OCR of Adjarian's *Dictionary of Armenian Personal Names* (Ačaṙyan, 1942–1962) by Calfa, which should result in a suitable, if incomplete, dataset of anthroponyms.

A number of annotated corpora are already freely available on the web, such as (Arak-29, since 2002) for Classical Armenian (mainly) or (EANC, 2006–2009) for Modern Eastern Armenian. Nevertheless, Ancient Armenian, generally speaking, remains an under-resourced language. Corpora featuring high-quality lexical tagging and available through interoperable formats are still scarce (Vidal-Gorène and Kindt, 2022; Vidal-Gorène and Decours-Perez, 2020). By processing this corpus, the GREgORI Project, in close connection with Calfa and the UCLouvain, intends to build up its linguistic resources and tailor them to the particular idiom of colophons, a task which is not only essential to a successful study of this textual content, but also paves the way for future research on other medieval Armenian sources.

6. Acknowledgements

Emmanuel Van Elverdinghe is a Postdoctoral Researcher of the Fonds de la Recherche Scientifique – FNRS.

Special thanks are due to Professor Bernard Coulie (UCLouvain), to Gabriel Kepeklian (UCLouvain), who manages the GREgORI Project's Armenian resources, and to Chahan Vidal-Gorène (Calfa), who is responsible for implementing an RNN model trained with the data of the GREgORI Project.

7. Bibliographical References

Ačaṙyan, H. (1942–1962). *Hayocʻ anjnanunneri baṙaran* [= *A Dictionary of Armenian Personal Names*], 5 vols. Erevan: Petakan hamalsarani hratarakčʻutʻyun.

Auer, P. and Schmidt, J. E. (Eds.). (2010). *Language and Space: An International Handbook of Linguistic Variation. Volume 1: Theories and Methods*. Berlin, New York: De Gruyter Mouton.

Coulie, B., Kindt, B., Kepeklian, G., and Van Elverdinghe, E. (2022). Étiquettes morphosyntaxiques et flexionnelles pour le traitement automatique de l'arménien ancien. *Le Muséon*, 135(1–2): 207–239.

Ghukasyan, Ts. *et al.* (2018), pioNER: Datasets and Baselines for Armenian Named Entity Recognition. In A. Avetisyan *et al.* (Eds.), *2018 Ivannikov Isp Ras Open Conference, Dedicated to the 70th Anniversary of Computer Science in Russia. ISPRAS 2018, 22–23 November 2018, Moscow, Russia Federation: Proceedings*, pp. 56–61. Los Alamitos, Washington, and Tokyo: IEEE Computer Society Conference Publishing Services.

Goepp, M., Mutafian, C., and Ouzounian, A. (2012). L'inscription du régent Constantin de Papeṙōn (1241). Redécouverte, relecture, remise en contexte historique. *Revue des études arméniennes*, 34: 243–287.

Hakobyan, Tʻ. X., Melikʻ-Bašxyan, St. T., and Barsełyan, H. X. (1986–2001). *Hayastani ev harakicʻ šrǰanneri tełanunneri baṙaran* [= *Dictionary of Toponymy of Armenia and Adjacent Territories*], 5 vols. Yerevan: Erevani hamalsarani hratarakčʻutʻyun.

Harutʻyunyan, X. (2014a). Holovman hamakargə XV dari hayeren jeṙagreri hišatakarannerum. *Banber Erevani Hamalsarani. Hasarakakan Gitutʻyunner. Šarkʻ 2. Banasirutʻiwn* [= The System of Declension in the Colophons of Armenian Manuscripts of the XV Century. *Bulletin of Yerevan University. Social Sciences. Volume 2: Philology*], 5(143): 123–131.

Harutʻyunyan, X. (2014b). XIV-XV dareri hayeren jeṙagreri hišatakaranneri lezvi hnčʻyunakan himnakan bnutʻagirə. *Banber Matenadarani* [= An Elementary Phonetic Description of the Language of Armenian Colophons of the 14th–15th Centuries. *Bulletin of Matenadaran*], 20, 175–187.

Harutʻyunyan, X. (2018a). Anjnanunnerə hayeren jeṙagreri hišatakarannerum. 1. Norahayt anjnanunner ŽA.-ŽG. dareri hišatakarannericʻ. *Banber Matenadarani* [= Personal Names in the Colophons of Armenian Manuscripts. 1: Newfound Personal Names in Colophons of the 11th–13th Centuries. *Bulletin of Matenadaran*], 25: 187–217.

Harutʻyunyan, X. (2018b). *Deł* armatov baładrvac anjnanunnerə vimagrerum ev jeṙagreri hišatakarannerum. In *Eritasardakan 3-rd gitažołovi zekucʻumner (Erevan, 2017 tʻ., noyemberi 28-30)* [= Personal Names with the Root *deł* in Armenian Colophons and Inscriptions. In *Papers of the III Youth Conference (Yerevan, 2017, November 28-30)*], pp. 115–133. Yerevan: Armav hratarakčʻutʻyun.

Harutʻyunyan, X. A. (2019). *Hayeren jeṙagreri hišatakarannerə* [= *The Colophons of Armenian Manuscripts*]. Yerevan: Matenadaran.

Hovsepʻyan, L. S. (1997). *ŽG dari hayeren jeṙagreri hišatakaranneri lezun* [= *The Language of the Armenian Colophons of the 13th Century*]. Yerevan: «Van Aryan» hratarakčʻatun.

J̌ahukyan, G. B. (1997). *Barbaṙayin erevuytʻnerə haykakan hišatakarannerum* [= *Dialect Features in Armenian Colophons*]. Yerevan: «Van Aryan» hratarakčʻatun.

Karst, J. (1901). *Historische Grammatik des Kilikisch-Armenischen*. Strasbourg: Verlag von Karl J. Trübner.

Kindt, B., Vidal-Gorène, Ch., and Delle Donne, S. (2022). Analyse automatique du grec ancien par réseau de neurones. Évaluation sur le corpus *De Thessalonica Capta*. *BABELAO*, 10–11: 537–562.

Margaryan, Al. S. (1993). Norahayt baṙer hayeren jeṙagreri XIV—XV dd. hišatakarannerum. *Patmabanasirakan handes* [= Newfound Words in the Colophons of Armenian Manuscripts of the 14th–15th Centuries. *Historical-Philological Journal*], 1–2(137–138): 35–42.

Matʻevosyan, A. S. (1984). *Hayeren jeṙagreri hišatakaranner. ŽG dar* [= *Colophons of Armenian Manuscripts: 13th Century*]. Yerevan: Haykakan SSH Gitutʻyunneri Akademiayi hratarakčʻutʻyun.

Stone, M. E. (1995). Colophons in Armenian Manuscripts. In E. Condello and G. De Gregorio (Eds.), *Scribi e colofoni. Le sottoscrizioni di copisti dalle origini all'avvento della stampa. Atti del seminario di Erice. X Colloquio del Comité international de paléographie latine (23-28 ottobre 1993)*, pp. 463–

471. Spoleto: Centro italiano di studi sull'alto medioevo.
Van Elverdinghe, E. (2018). Recurrent Pattern Modelling in a Corpus of Armenian Manuscript Colophons. *Journal of Data Mining and Digital Humanities, Special Issue on Computer-Aided Processing of Intertextuality in Ancient Languages*, 8 pp.
Van Elverdinghe, E. (2022). *Modèles et copies. Étude d'une formule des colophons de manuscrits arméniens, VIIIe-XIXe siècles*. Louvain: Peeters.
Vidal-Gorène, Ch. and Decours-Perez, A. (2020). Languages Resources for Poorly Endowed Languages: The Case Study of Classical Armenian. In N. Calzolari *et al.* (Eds.), *LREC 2020, Marseille. Twelfth International Conference on Language Resources and Evaluation, May 11-16, 2020, Palais du Pharo, Marseille, France: Conference proceedings*, pp. 3145–3152. Paris: The European Language Resources Association (ELRA).
Vidal-Gorène, Ch. and Kindt, B. (2020). Lemmatization and POS-tagging process by using joint learning approach. Experimental results on Classical Armenian, Old Georgian, and Syriac. In R. Sprugnoli and M. Passarotti (Eds.), *1st Workshop on Language Technologies for Historical and Ancient Languages, (LT4HALA 2020): Proceedings*, pp. 22–27. Paris: European Language Resources Association (ELRA).
Vidal-Gorène, Ch. and Kindt, B. (2022). From manuscript to tagged corpora. An automated process for Ancient Armenian or other under resourced languages of the Christian East. *Armeniaca*, 1, submitted.
Weitenberg, J. J. S. (1995). The Role of Morphologic Variation in Medieval Armenian Poetry. In J. J. S. Weitenberg (Ed.), *New Approaches to Medieval Armenian Language and Literature*, pp. 121–134. Amsterdam, Atlanta (GA): Rodopi.
Weitenberg, J. J. S. (2005). Cultural Interaction in the Middle East as Reflected in the Anthroponomy of Armenian 12th – 14th Century Colophons. In J. J. van Ginkel, H. L. Murre-van den Berg, and Th. M. van Lint (Eds.), *Redefining Christian Identity: Cultural Interaction in the Middle East since the Rise of Islam*, pp. 265–263. Louvain, Paris, Dudley (MA): Uitgeverij Peeters; Departement Oosterse Studies.
Xačʻikyan, L., Matʻevosyan, A., and Łazarosyan, A. (2018). *Hayeren jeṙagreri hišatakaranner. ŽD dar. Masn A (1301-1325 tʻtʻ.)* [= *Colophons of Armenian Manuscripts: 14th Century. Part 1 (1301–1325)*]. Yerevan: «Nairi» hratarakčʻutʻyun.
Xačʻikyan, L., Matʻevosyan, A., and Łazarosyan, A. (2020). *Hayeren jeṙagreri hišatakaranner. ŽD dar. Masn B (1326-1350 tʻtʻ.)* [= *Colophons of Armenian Manuscripts: 14th Century. Part 2 (1326–1350)*]. Yerevan: Matenadaran.
Xačʻikyan, L. S. (1950). *ŽD dari hayeren jeṙagreri hišatakaranner* [= *Colophons of Armenian Manuscripts of the 14th Century*]. Yerevan: Haykakan SSṘ Gitutʻyunneri Akademiayi hratarakčʻutʻyun.
Xačʻikyan, L. S. (1955). *ŽE dari hayeren jeṙagreri hišatakaranner. Masn aṙajin (1401—1450 tʻtʻ.)* [= *Colophons of Armenian Manuscripts of the 15th Century. First Part (1401–1450)*]. Yerevan: Haykakan SSṘ Gitutʻyunneri Akademiayi Hratarakčʻutʻyun.
Xačʻikyan, L. S. (1967). *ŽE dari hayeren jeṙagreri hišatakaranner. Masn errord (1481—1500 tʻtʻ.)* [= *Colophons of Armenian Manuscripts of the 15th Century. Third Part (1481–1500)*]. Yerevan: Haykakan SSH Gitutʻyunneri Akademiayi hratarakčʻutʻyun.

8. Language Resource References

Arak-29. (since 2002). Առակ-29 / Arak-29. Առակ-29 կրթամշակութային հիմնադրամ, https://arak29.org.
Calfa. (since 2014). Calfa, https://calfa.fr.
EANC. (2006–2009). Eastern Armenian National Corpus. Corpus Technologies, http://www.eanc.net.
GREgORI Project. (since 1990). GREgORI – Software, linguistic data and tagged corpora for ancient GREek and ORIental languages, https://uclouvain.be/fr/instituts-recherche/incal/ciol/gregori-project.html, ISSN 2736-7657 (Bernard Coulie, Academic supervisor).
pioNER. (2018). pioNER - named entity annotated datasets and GloVe models for the Armenian language, https://github.com/ispras-texterra/pioner.

9. Appendix: samples of concordances

9.1 Concordance of the lemma բերդ *berd* (fortress) in the sub-corpus

բերդ { N+Com } (9)

XIV_B 670 0 296 9	ոչ մարդութիւն յետ այնոց, որ ի	բերդերն	ի փախուստ էին
XIV_B 670 0 296 8	ի սովոյ, որ չմնաց շէն յետ ի	բերդերոյն,	զոր մնացին, ոչ մարդութիւն
XIV_B 670 0 296 2	երետ, զոր կտրէր Ջահան՝	բերդերովն	ու զերկիրն ու զպանծալին՝ Այաս,
XV_A 347 0 328 11	յայն տարին որ զՎանայ	բերդն	առին ի քրդուն Սքանդար ամիրզէն,
XIV_B 670 0 295 28	Այթուն Պուղայս արգել զմեզ ի Հալպա	բերդն	ի զնդան:
XV_A 580 0 515 10	Ջահանշէն, որ զԼոռու	բերդն	հեսարեց՝ սուրբ աւետարանս զերի անկօ:
XV_A 330 0 314 8	բազում հեծելօք, եւ զՎանայ	բերդս	խսարեաց, եւ շատ աւեր էած,
XIV 647 0 521 20	աւարումն եղաւ Լամ[բ]րոն	բե[ր]թի,	եւ գերի բերին ըզսուրբ աւետարանս
XIV_B 670 0 295 24	մալին առնելոյն սուլտանին ուզեց	զբերդերն,	զգետին այն դեհին, զոր այլ էր տված:

9.2 Concordance of the lemma տամ *tam* (to give) in the sub-corpus

տամ { V } (40)

XIV_A 437 3 492 26	ի ծառայութենէ այլազգեաց, եւ	ետ	Գէորգ վարդապետին,
XIV_A 111 3 121 8	ի ձեռաց անօրինաց եւ	ետ	դարձեալ ի դուռն Սուրբ Խաչին
XV_A 699 0 619 37	զկենակիցն Շախփաշայ [...] որ	ետ	երկու գրիւ ցորէն
XIV 681 0 546 11	եւ զպակասն գրել	ետ	եւ եդ ի գեղ Կախմխին,
XV_A 1 0n1 3n 13	Փափաքեցաւ սուրբ աւետարանիս,	ետ	զիւր հացի գին
XV_A 585 2 519 5	[...]: եւ	ետ	զսայ ընծայ սուրբ Աստուածածնիս
XV_A 699 0 619 38	զզանձարանս ի գերութենէ, եւ	ետ	ի դուռն սուրբ Աստուածածնին,
XV_A 585 1 518 21	մահդասիս Ամիր-Փաշա, եւ	ետ	ի հալալ արդեանց իւրոց
XIV 593 4 485 5	ի ձեռաց անօրինաց եւ	ետ	ծաղկել զսա:
XIV_B 670 0 295 16	գնեալ զսա եւ բերեալ յերկիրս, եւ	ետ	յանարժան ծառայս Աստուծոյ
XV_A 585 2 519 16	մահդասի Ամիր-Փաշայ անուն էառ՝	ետ	սուրբ առաքեալն Թադէոսի:
XIV_B 799 0 447 10	գնեց զսայ ի յարդար ընչից իւրոց եւ	ետ	վերըստին ի Սուրբ Կարապետս
XIV_B 821 0 488 9	եւ ի վաստակոց […] եւ	ետ	վերստին ծաղկել եւ կազմել զսա […]:
XIV 685 0 549 25	եւ իմ սրտի աւժարութեամբս	ետու	զայս ի գերեզման սուրբ Մեսրոպ
XIV 679 1 545 6	բերի ի Տրապիզոնս եւ	ետու	ի Չարխափան սուրբ Աստուածածինս:
XIV 649 0 523 8	գնեցի ի գերողէն, եւ	ետու	ի սուրբ ուխտն ի սուրբ Աստուածածին
XV_A 347 0 328 14	գնեցի զսա ի հալալ արդեանց իմոց եւ	ետու	ի սուրբ ուխտն Վերի Վարագ,
XIV 676 0 543 8	եւ սէր ցուցանելով, <եւ>	ետու	Ճ դ[ահե]կ[ան], այլ եւ թափեցի
XV_A 136 0 134 14	ըստ աստուածասէր բարուց իւրեանց	ետուն	զգին եւ ազատեցին ի գերութենէ:
XV_A 330 0 314 13	[...]: եւ	ետուն	ի գին նորա ՌԵՃ դր[ամ] մերտնցի,
XV_A 136 0 134 15	եւ դարձեալ	ետուն	ծախք եւ ետուն կազմել
XV_A 136 0 134 15	եւ դարձեալ ետուն ծախք եւ	ետուն	կազմել զսուրբ աւետարանս
XV_A 330 0 314 14	ՌԵՃ դր[ամ] մերտնցի, եւ	ետուն	կրկին ի սուրբ ուխտն [...]
XIV_B 670 0 296 1	կատարեաց զսուլտանին կամքն ու	երետ,	զոր կտրէր Ջահան՝
XV_A 585 2 519 23	առեալ էր՝ զամէնն	էրետ	եւ գնեց զաստուածային գանձս,
XV_A 585 2 519 19	Յովանէս զիւր հոգոյ բաժինն	էրետ	եւ էառ զսա յիշատակ հոգոյ իւրոյ,
XIV 592 0 484 4	ի Մ եւ Ծ դ[ահե]կ[ան], զապականացուն	տալով	զանանցն ստացան:
XV_A 418 1 392 14	Սարգսին, զոր տէր աստուած վայելել	տացէ	ընդ երկայն աւուրս:
XIV_B 670 0 295 31	որոյ ողորմեսցի Տէր Յիսուս եւ	տացէ	իր պսակ մարտիրոսական,
XIV 676 0 543 11	զոր տէր աստուած վայելել	տացէ	խորին ծերութեամբն,
XIV 593 4 485 5	Որոյ տէր աստուած վայելել	տացէ	նմա բազում ժամանակս,
XV_A 307 0 296 2	եւ մեք այլ յիւր տեղն	տըւինք,	ՊՀԱ: [...]
XV_A 580 0 515 12	կանգնեցաք Ռ դեկան	տուաք,	թափեցաք ի գերութենէ
XV_A 307 0 295 39	որ էր գերի [...] այլասեռաց. եւ	տուաք	ի սուրբ ուխտն՝ ի Տկուց վանքն,
XV_A 418 2 392 21	Ես Բեշքէն, որդի պարոն Սմպատին	տուի	մեզ արեւշատութեան
XIV_B 670 0 295 21	սուլտանն ընդ ձեզ սէր է,	տուք	զմալն ու խառ խասատ մի մալ՝
XIV_B 670 0 295 24	զգետին այն դեհին, զոր այլ էր	տված:	Նայ՝ արքայն Լեւոն առաքեաց
XIV 685 0 549 22	ու Ա կապոց Ճ դ[ահե]կ[ա]նի՝	տվի	ի յիմ հալալ արդեանց
XV_A 87 0 89 26	եւ իմ հալալ արդեանց	տվի	Մ դեկան, եւ թափեցի
XV_A 418 2 392 27	որ մեր Դաւայքարու տէր՝	տւինք	ի յեկեղեցին Սիւնէվանից,

Proceedings of the Workshop on Processing Language Variation: Digital Armenian (DigitAm 2022) @LREC2022, pages 28–37
Marseille, 20 June 2022

Eastern Armenian National Corpus: State of the Art and Perspectives

Victoria Khurshudyan, Timofey Arkhangelskiy, Michael Daniel, Dmitri Levonian, Vladimir Plungian, Alex Polyakov, Sergei Rubakov
INALCO/SeDyL/CNRS/IRD, Universität Hamburg, School of Linguistics / Linguistic Convergence Laboratory, HSE University, Corpus Technologies, Russian Academy of Sciences, Corpus Technologies
65 rue des Grands Moulins, 75013 Paris
victoria.khurshudyan@inalco.fr, timofey.arkhangelskiy@uni-hamburg.de, misha.daniel@gmail.com, dlevonian@gmail.com, plungian@gmail.com, pollex@mail.ru, rubakov@gmail.com

Abstract
Eastern Armenian National Corpus (EANC) is a comprehensive corpus of Modern Eastern Armenian with about 110 million tokens, covering written and oral discourses from the mid-19th century to the present. The corpus is provided with morphological, semantic and metatext annotation, as well as English translations. EANC is open access and available at www.eanc.net.

Keywords: Armenian, corpus linguistics, annotation

1. Introduction

Corpus linguistics (McEnery and Wilsonn, 2001; 2012; Stefanowitsch, 2020; i.a.) started to develop actively only from 1990-ies with the evolution of new technologies facilitating the compilation and processing of different types of corpora. Corpus linguistics is based on empirical data and reflects the language reality throughout all forms of language production.

In corpus linguistics a corpus is defined as a set of texts, and a reference corpus as a balanced and representative set of texts (written discourse) and/or transcripts (oral discourse) varied by different parameters (genre, chronology, original and translated literature etc.), provided by various types of annotation (metatextual, morphological, syntactical etc.) and searchable by various linguistic or pragmatic criteria.

Despite being a language with a multisecular written tradition, Armenian[1] is an under-resource language and it lacks significantly digital resources for Natural language Processing (NLP) and linguistic research. Several rare projects for particular Armenian varieties exist, as well as a growing interest in NLP resources is observed.

General purpose untagged Armenian plain texts are represented by a number of open-access online libraries in the Internet offering mainly fiction and press (for a more detailed overview on the existing resources for different Armenian varieties see (Vidal-Gorene et al., 2020)). Often the available data are merely scanned rather than OCRed.

At the time of Eastern Armenian National Corpus (EANC) launching (2006) the availability of Modern Eastern Armenian (MEA) data was quite inadequate with only few e-libraries offering popular fiction with an estimated total volume of about 1 million words. In the available open online resources, non-fiction genres (except press) were often missing. MEA press enjoys better online representation mostly due to online editions of a number of popular Armenian newspapers.

More recently MEA project of Universal Dependencies provides a treebank of about 50K tokens (2502 sentences) with morphological and syntactic annotations in the form of a dependency tree bank (Yavrumyan, 2020; Yavrumyan and Danielyan, 2020).

Currently, several other resources provide MEA plain-text or scanned databases (Armenian Wikipedia and Wikisource (about 50M tokens), Fundamental Scientific Library of the National Academy of Sciences of the Republic of Armenia[2] (considerable number of scanned books of different genres as well as press archives), etc.). Rare tools such as spellcheckers and orthography converters exist for the two modern standards. More recently, some NLP research projects have been conducted to address particular NLP issues, such as named entity recognition (Ghukasyan et al., 2018), word embeddings (Avetisyan and Ghukasyan, 2019) or paraphrase detection for Armenian (Malajyan et al., 2020).

Russian National Corpus[3] provides an aligned sub-corpus of MEA and Russian on the basis of the translated texts existing in EANC. The sub-corpus is

[1] The Armenian language in all its variation encompasses Classical Armenian (5th-10th cen. A.D), preserved exclusively for canonical uses, Middle Armenian (11th-17th cen.), and Modern Armenian (17th cen. – up to present) with its two standards: Modern Eastern Armenian (the official language of the Republic of Armenia, which is also the language of the Armenian communities of Iran and the ex-Soviet republics) and Modern Western Armenian (spoken by traditional Armenian communities in Europe, the Americas and the Middle East originating mainly from the Ottoman Empire), both standardized in the 19th cen. Aside from the two standards, the Armenian language continuum includes various dialects, as well as vernacular forms. All the written varieties of the Armenian language use the unique Armenian alphabet.

[2] https://arar.sci.am/

[3] https://ruscorpora.ru/new/search-para.html?lang=hye

provided with full morphological annotation for both languages and it covers about 2,4M tokens.
In contrast to the written discourse, MEA oral data is rarely available for research. During the last years several projects elaborating MEA Automatic speech recognition (ASR) models[4] came out.
As of today, EANC is the largest Armenian resource.

1. EANC Overview

The project of Eastern Armenian National Corpus (www.eanc.net) was launched in 2006 (the current version corresponding to the third release as of 2009) by a group of linguists and it was supported by Corpus Technologies, a Moscow-based NLP development company.
EANC is designed as a comprehensive corpus with about 110 million tokens, covering Modern Eastern Armenian written and oral discourses from the mid-19th century to the present. The texts/transcripts have morphological, semantic and metatext annotation and they are provided by English translations for frequent tokens searchable for making complex lexical morphological queries. EANC is an open access corpus available at www.eanc.net. EANC proposes also an electronic library (scanned and processed entirely by the EANC team) with full-view access for over hundreds of works by classical authors in public domain. The library provides the same morphological analysis and translation as the rest of the corpus (displayed on mouse click). Due to copyright considerations, the search function in the main corpus does not provide access to the texts in their entirety.
The term "national", included in the name of EANC, has a terminological rather than emotional value. After British National Corpus[5], the concept of a "national corpus" has come to designate a comprehensive and representative corpus of a language: cf. Russian National Corpus[6], Czech National Corpus[7], Georgian National Corpus[8], among others. It is in this sense that the Eastern Armenian National Corpus qualifies as a national corpus of a language.

2. EANC Composition

EANC is designed as a comprehensive corpus with the objective to include as many MEA texts as practicable – all literary, scientific and oral texts available to us have been indexed for search. The only exception to this is certain widely-available texts, such as electronic press and legal documents, whose presence has been limited for the sake of balance among different genres.
Due to its comprehensive nature, EANC is inherently different from the high-resource languages' corpora such as Russian National Corpus or British National Corpus which choose their collections selectively. BNC additionally imposes a limit on the number of words per document, truncating longer texts. EANC, on the other hand, includes a great majority of all extant Eastern Armenian literary texts. In this respect, EANC is similar to Czech National Corpus, Slovak National Corpus[9] or Georgian National Corpus.
The vast majority of EANC written texts except press are obtained through scanning and OCRing scanned materials using ABBYY Fine Reader 8.0. Most of the EANC press corpus was downloaded from open electronic archives of the newspapers that provide access to such archives (e.g. www.azg.am, www.aravot.am, www.yerkir.am, www.iravunk.com etc.).

Written discourse	# tokens	% EANC	# of docs
Fiction			
prose: novels	29 729 521	27,1%	366
prose: short stories	5 888 695	5,4%	158
prose: plays	1 411 030	1,3%	55
prose subtotal	**37 029 246**	**33,7%**	**579**
poetry	3 627 119	3,3%	208
Press	47 264 735	43,0%	7858
Non-fiction			
science	13 750 358	12,5%	112
essays, memoirs, official, religious	4 680 539	4,3%	360
Written total	**106 351 997**	**96,8%**	**9 117**
Oral discourse	**# tokens**	**% EANC**	**# of docs**
Oral spontaneous discourse	1 029 646	0,94%	208
Oral public discourse	1 933 899	1,76%	543
Oral task-oriented discourse	70 010	0,06%	22
+ Online communication	442 399	0,40%	1
Oral total	**3 475 954**	**3,2%**	**774**
EANC Total	**109 827 951**	**100%**	**9 891**

Table 1: EANC composition by genre

About 1 million tokens of texts have been downloaded from public electronic collections (www.armenianhouse.org, www.hayeren.hayastan.com etc.).

EANC includes written texts of various genres (over 106M tokens) such as fiction, press, poetry, non-fiction, etc., as well as a diversified corpus of oral speech (about 3,5M tokens) (see Table 1).
EANC includes not only all school reading texts in today's Armenian secondary school program, but the vast majority of MEA classical literature starting from mid-19th century, a large number of scientific texts (including the 13-volume Armenian Soviet Encyclopaedia 1974-1987).

4 MEA ASR model by Public initiative for national acceleration (https://arm.ican24.net/demoasrv4.html), Mozilla common voice project for MEA (https://pontoon.mozilla.org/hy-AM/common-voice/), MEA ASR model integrated in Google translate (https://translate.google.com/?hl=hy&sl=hy&tl=la&op=translate), Sonix's MEA model https://sonix.ai/languages/transcribe-armenian-audio, https://hindityping.info/speech-to-text/armenian/.
5 www.natcorp.ox.ac.uk
6 www.ruscorpora.ru
7 https://ucnk.ff.cuni.cz
8 http://gnc.gov.ge
9 https://korpus.sk

Each of the 9,960 document entries in EANC is labeled by metatext information specifying genre and other bibliographic details (e.g. date of creation/publication, name of the author, etc.).

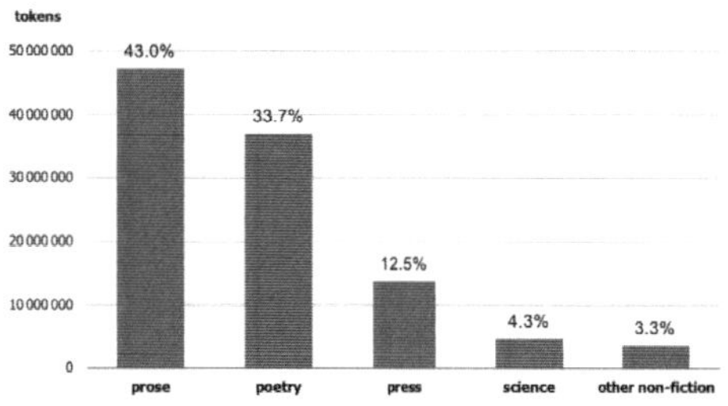

Figure 1: EANC written discourse composition

Written discourse sub-corpus in EANC includes over 106 million tokens covering over 500 authors, a sizeable collection of press, scientific and other non-fiction texts, as well as some 130 translated texts.
Various genres of EANC texts are distributed unevenly over time. The 19th and 20th centuries are mostly represented by literary texts, prose and poetry. Some older press has been added to the corpus in a joined project by EANC and the Armenian National Library to render the press sub-corpus more balanced chronologically. The main bulk of the press sub-corpus, however, was acquired by downloading texts from open newspaper archives and thus represents the modern (from 2000 on) language of internet news resources of the Republic of Armenia. This makes the ratio between press and fiction texts for the last decade very different from the same ratio for the rest of the corpus.
Oral discourse sub-corpus (about 3,5M tokens) is an important part of EANC represented by spontaneous dialogs, polylogs, task-oriented interviews, TV talk shows, movies, and other recordings, all transcribed by EANC.
The oral discourse sub-corpus of the EANC being a linguistic and corpus project on its own, it is impertinent to implement any balance restrictions controlling the proportion of written vs. oral discourse (unlike within the written corpus where a reasonable balance is required between various genres and types of texts).

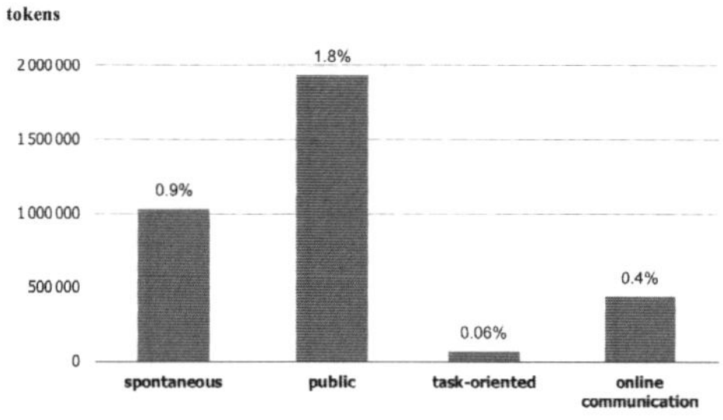

Figure 2: EANC oral discourse composition

Oral discourse in EANC is represented by the Yerevan standard which is justified by the fact that it is the closest spoken dialect to Modern Eastern Armenian, the language of the written sub-corpus and which historically served as a spoken prototype for the MEA literary tradition. The entire oral discourse corpus has been recorded and transcribed within the framework of the EANC project.
Oral public discourse (about 2M tokens) is originally recorded in video format and includes various recordings of TV programs, talk shows, public debates, interviews, etc. broadcasted by Armenian TV stations. Audio data are then extracted and stored as audio files. Oral spontaneous discourse and task-oriented discourse are recorded in audio format (.mp3 or .wav). The respondents are speakers of the Yerevan standard and are selected in an attempt to obtain a balanced mix of age, gender, and social status. The corpus of oral spontaneous discourse (over 1M tokens) includes spontaneous polylogues, dialogues and diverse narratives. The corpus of task-oriented discourse (about 70,000 tokens) covers favorite film narratives and cartoon narratives.
Currently, EANC oral discourse corpus uses a *plain* transcription which basically follows traditional Armenian orthography and punctuation standards. Only few additional special tags are used: == for falsestarts, = for fragmented words, among other tags.

3. Annotation and Grammatical Wordlist EANC Composition

All the annotation information enhances the EANC search capability by allowing the user to build and search sub-corpora and to sort the search results. Three major layers of markup are implemented in EANC:
1. *Metatext (bibliographic) markup* is assigned to each text unit and includes such metatext information as author, title, year of creation, and genre (genres) etc.
2. *Token markup* includes lexical and morphological markup assigned to over 90% of tokens as well as English translations for about 85% of tokens. Every token (wordform) in EANC is supplied with a set of lexical morphological tags (labels). These tags cover grammatical categories applicable to MEA (part of speech, case, number, determination, tense-aspect-mood, polarity, inflection type etc.). EANC tagging system follows the Leipzig Glossing Rules (as of 2015)[10] as closely as possible (see Annexe 1: EANC grammatical tags). Few solutions have been made that may appear controversial, but these are mainly connected to controversial or understudied phenomena in Armenian grammar itself (such as interpretating dative / genitive and destinative / dative infinitive syncretism or the morphological composition of relational forms of nouns, such as *սեղանինր*).
3. The third markup layer covers *punctuation, sentence boundaries, and auxiliary markup options.*
Linguistic background of the project comprises two main components – the wordlist and a morphological model (inflectional classification).

[10] https://www.eva.mpg.de/lingua/pdf/Glossing-Rules.pdf

The EANC wordlist is based on a combination of the wordlist of E. Galstian's Armenian-Russian dictionary (1985) and part of E. Aghaian's dictionary of Modern Armenian (1976) (over 70,000 entries), the wordlist of H. Grgearian and N. Harutyunian's dictionary of geographic names (1987-1989) (about 4,000 entries), a list of common first names and family names (about 1000 entries), abbreviation wordlist from D. Gyurdjinian and N. Hekekian's dictionary of acronyms used in Armenian (2007) (about 2000 entries). Additionally, the EANC wordlist includes a limited number of lexemes, such as neologisms, that occur in EANC but are missing from the sources above. Such lexemes were added manually on the basis of the list of non-annotated words filtered by their frequency in EANC.

To make lemmatization possible a morphological model with a formal and exhaustive classification of MEA inflection types for both nominal and verbal categories was worked out. Each inflectable lexeme in the EANC wordlist was then assigned a specific tag corresponding to the relevant inflection type (e.g. N11, N12, V11, V12 etc.).

Comprising a wordlist and providing an internationally-compatible inventory of morphological categories was mainly a technical task. The main challenge has been to work out a formal morphological model of Modern Eastern Armenian inflection that would be comprehensive enough to cover most of the corpus tokens. In other words, each lexeme that inflects had to be provided with information about its paradigmatic type (or types, in case of inflectional variance) that predicts its forms. This challenge may seem unexpected, provided a long tradition of Armenian studies. However, the conventional grammars of Eastern Armenian proved not to be formal enough for an automatic analysis (lemmatization) of EANC electronic library, which is quite justifiable because conventional grammars serve a purpose other than automatic processing (mostly educational).

By way of example, the current inflectional classification of MEA nouns used in EANC includes 45 types, nine of which could be considered as subtypes and grouped into nine larger classes, which roughly correspond to conventional declensions. Some types are different from others by vowel reduction or, for nouns, plural formation, which cross-cuts the whole system of MEA nominal inflection; some classes are not real declensions, being limited to few lexemes only. The full list of types is available at the project site and covers all or, strictly speaking, all we are currently aware of, types of paradigms that have at least one position that distinguishes it from all other types of paradigms. Similar classifications have been elaborated for pronouns and verbs.

The inflectional classification of MEA applied is based on orthography, and, thus, more of an applied linguistic than a purely linguistic project (although a speech-oriented linguistic classification may be obtained relatively easily).

Figure 3:

One of the challenges has been analysing orthographic variants[11] widespread in MEA texts, including old writings or Western Armenian inserts. The markup was designed to allow to find regular and deviant orthographic variants in one same query, as well as tokens using non-standard orthography.

Supplemented with part-of-speech and inflectional information, the EANC wordlist became a grammatical e-

dictionary, similar to those used by Internet search engines for other morphologically rich languages.

4. Software

EANC database software consists of four major parts: parser, indexer, server and user interface and client.

The collection of raw electronic texts is first processed by EANC *Parser* (a PERL program), which adds XML-compliant or tab-delimited metatext and token markup. Next, the resulting files are processed by the *Indexer* to create the corpus database structure. *Server* implements search and sorting algorithms in the corpus database. Finally, *User interface* and *Client* provide web access to the EANC database and its search functionality.

The EANC Parser assigns token markup tags to each wordform, provided that the respective lexeme is present in the EANC grammatical wordlist. Overall, 92,5% of all tokens are recognized and annotated with 72,6% analyzed unambiguously, 17% ambiguously, and 7,5% not recognized. Parsing success rate varies depending on a genre. The highest percentage of unrecognized tokens occurs, unsurprisingly, in oral discourse.

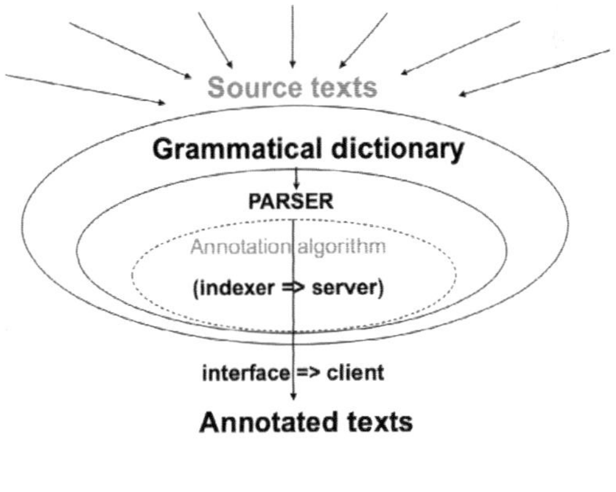

Figure 3: EANC database software

Some wordforms have multiple analysis. For example, the forms for infinitive and perfective converb in MEA are regularly homonymous for the *-ե* (-e) conjugation

[11] Up to the 1920s both MEA and Modern Western Armenian (MWA) together with Classical Armenian had a common spelling. Once Armenia was sovietised an orthography reform was made with the objective of simplification and rendering it more phonetic, though political reasons were certainly not of last importance either. Currently, classical spelling is used for MWA and by the Armenian community in Iran for MEA, whereas reformed spelling is applied in Armenia and other Eastern Armenian communities.

type (*գրել grel* 'to write'). An example of an occasional homonymy is *հարգի hargi* 'respectable': it is analyzed both as an adjective and as a subjunctive, 3rd person, present of the verb *հարգել hargel* 'to respect'. This lexical morphological homonymy, both regular and coincidental, is quite common in MEA, the overall percentage of tokens with multiple analysis being as high as about 12%. Currently, EANC parser deals exclusively with the wordform, completely ignoring their context. The noise level can be cut down by adding specific constraints to the query, e.g. by introducing another wordform that is supposed to co-occur with the relevant reading.

Indexer is a PHP+MySQL program that extracts address information for each token and each markup element from the XML output provided by the *EANC Parser*. The output of *Indexer* is a set of hash tables that establish a pointer connection between each unique lexeme, wordform and grammatical attribute occurring in EANC, and their respective positions (addresses) in the corpus data files. The corpus data files represent a non-relational database consisting of binary address arrays. Sorting keys for each token are also stored in the data files. This allows sorting output contexts by specific key criteria, such as alphabetically, by period/genre, etc.

Server is a C++ program which implements core search algorithms over the corpus data files via the ISAM method. Search algorithms are designed to minimize response time for most common queries. Given the size of EANC (well over 100M tokens), response time may exceed the standard 0.5-0.8 second threshold for some contextual queries such as searching for complex collocation sequences of frequent gram attributes.

Many queries may correspond to a large number of matches in EANC; however, only up to 10,000 matches are displayed to the user. These 10,000 are drawn from various parts of the Corpus proportionally to the way *all* matches are distributed throughout EANC, so as to form a representative sample (if a sub-corpus has been defined, the same distribution sampling is performed over the sub-corpus).

EANC user interface is a PHP/HTML program that provides user access to the full search functionality of the server. Visually, the user interface is a collection of browser windows, including: Search form appearing on the right side of the EANC web page, gram selection form, sub-corpus selection form, display options form, search output area and a number of auxiliary windows such as virtual Armenian keyboard.

The main search form is the central element of the EANC user interface. It is used to build various types of queries (e.g. for a lexeme or a wordform, gram attributes, punctuation, case-sensitivity etc.).

When the user defines a search query, the user interface transmits that query to *Client*. *Client* is a PHP program that pre-processes user input in the User interface, builds and sends a query to *Server*, and then receives and post-processes the search output. *Client* is also responsible for more advanced interface operations, such as displaying token markup or transliterating the output. The grammatical wordlist of MEA is used by the parser, EANC corpus software that ascribes each token a lexical morphological analysis.

Apart from the parser EANC software is designed as a scalable and a language-independent software platform for corpus studies. The system is built in a way that corpora of structurally different languages can be indexed and made available for search provided that such corpora follow the specific XML markup standards developed by Corpus Technologies (cf. in 2011-2017 EANC software was used for Albanian, Ossetic, Buryat, Mongolian, Kazakh corpora[12]).

Morphological analysis in general can be either rule-based or statistical. In case of statistical analysis certain amount of training data (100,000-1,000,000 words) is annotated manually on which a smart algorithm is trained which finally learns and provides the rules to annotate texts. One of the advantages of this method is the possibility to analyze previously unseen words, thus no dictionary is required. This mode of analysis is popular for large languages and the more fine-grained the tagset, the larger the training dataset is needed.

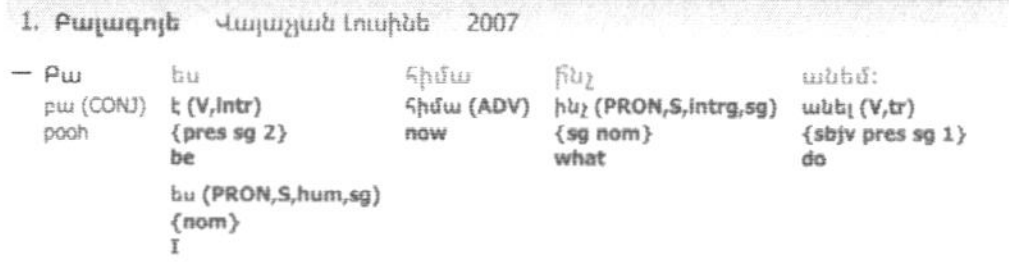

Figure 4: EANC annotated example

Current EANC morphological analysis is rule-based with manually compiled dictionary and morphological rules that the analyzer applies to the text. Such analysis results in ambiguous analyses since words are analyzed regardless of context and out-of-vocabulary words are not recognized. Rule-based analysis is advantageous for adding dictionary lexical information (e.g. translations, animacy, diathesis etc.) and it does not require training data. However, the description format is not really transparent, as it only provides grammatical tags rather than glossing, which is a standard in typology and many other linguistic subdisciplines.

Tagging + translation	**կփորձեն** attempt, feel, try (V,tr) cond,prs,pl,3
Glossing	կ-փորձ-են k-p'orj-en COND-attempt-SBJV.PRS.3PL

Figure 5: Example with standard typological glossing

By the initiative of Timofey Arkhangelskiy and Aleksei Fedorenko the existing analyzer was improved and updated. The rules of the analyzer were rewritten in a format allowing glossing (Uniparser); the vocabulary was converted automatically, whereas

[12] http://web-corpora.net/

the inflection was rewritten manually. Certain procedures were applied to prepare stem glosses. Importantly, the analyzer[13] is now open source (MIT license).
The analyzer was tested on about 10 million tokens from EANC. The test dataset included 19th and 20th century fiction, press, scientific literature, as well as oral discourse. The test proved 93% coverage (not including tokens in non-Armenian script) and 1,25 ambiguity analysis per analyzed word. The updated test dataset was published through *tsakorpus*[14] corpus platform. The objective is to move entire EANC to *tsakorpus*.

5. Search Functionality and Display Options

EANC was designed first as an instrument of linguistic analysis and thus has to provide efficient tools of looking for linguistic information.
EANC allows to make token queries by wordforms (e.g. *մարդու mardu 'man.SG.GEN'*), lexemes (e.g. *մարդ mard 'man.SG.NOM'*, *մարդու* ***mardu 'man.SG.GEN'***, *մարդիկ mardik 'man.PL.NOM'* and so on for the lexeme *մարդ* mard) or English translation (e.g. *man*) or queries based on a specific grammatical attribute or a combination of attributes (e.g. passive imperfective converbs or searching for *տուն tun 'house'* in singular definite yields such forms as nominative *տունը* tunə and *տունն* tunn, dative *տանը* tanə etc.).
Additional search criteria and options, such as case-sensitivity (e.g. capitalized tokens only), adjacent punctuation (only tokens preceding a comma) or position in the sentence (e.g. only tokens neither in the beginning nor in the end of a sentence) can be applied as well.
The most fascinating (and, in terms of software support, the most challenging) query option is a context query, a combination of several token queries. Using a context query, the use of the corpus may look for co-occurrences of tokens defined in each token query included in the context query in the same context. Co-occurrence is subject to distance limitations which may require that tokens occur next to each other (default option), at a distance between two values specified, simply within the same sentence, or in different sentences in the document.
Examples of context queries include, for instance, searching for a noun preceded by a genitive and an adjective, perfective converbs followed by any wordforms of the stative verb *է* with not more than one other wordform between them*, or co-occurrence of two negative verb forms in two adjacent sentences.
Further important search option is limiting the search domain to a subset of the texts of the corpus. The criteria might be the time of book creation, genres or types of texts, author or authors or the title of the book. The user may thus choose to look only for the matches occurring in Raffi's Samvel, in all Raffi's novels, in all novels of the 19-th century, or in all texts dating from the 19th century in general. This is extremely useful when e.g. trying to investigate semantic or other diachronical processes in the language, e.g. comparing the contexts using the verb *պրծացնել prcac'nel* 'finish' in the 19th and 20th centuries.
The display options allow to have the output in Armenian characters or in transliteration, to choose the layout (full (by default), light, glossed or KWIC), as well as extending the matches per page from 10 to 50 and the sentences in the context from 1 to 3.
The user can also choose the way in which the contexts matching the query are sorted, i.e. in what order they appear on the screen. Important sorting options are sorting alphabetically by the lexeme or wordform matching the query, by year of creation or by the name of the author (note that sorting criteria may be combined). Thus, sorting by the year of creation provides a convenient tool of observing the change of meaning of a word or use of a form over time.

6. Objective and Target Audience

Current state of Armenian studies requires new approaches and linguistic tools to validate key empirical hypotheses and findings as well as to expand the field of research. Corpus-based approach will allow revisiting the aspects of the traditional grammar that have not been sufficiently studied and will facilitate developing new descriptive and theoretical concepts.
EANC provides linguists with a searchable annotated database of MEA. EANC includes empirical linguistic data ranging from classical standard Eastern Armenian literature to Yerevan street talk recorded and transcribed in 2008.
EANC also provides a researcher with an option to build a user-defined sub-corpus, such as a single author sub-corpus, or a sub-corpus containing specific genres and/or periods.
Since EANC provides samples of actual MEA usage across periods, genres, and discourse formats, it can also be used as a powerful educational resource. English translations are provided for about 85 percent of the tokens, facilitating the use of the corpus by non-native speakers, e.g. Armenian language learners. EANC can also be used in various fields such as literature and culture studies, journalism, history, and others.
Importantly, EANC is as much about corpus linguistics as it is about Armenian studies. The EANC team aimed to build a modern flexible linguistic database that can be used as a platform for creating corpora of other languages, exploring statistical approaches to language description, as well as applying natural language processing methods.

7. Problems and Perspectives

A major problem of the EANC is the presence of numerous mistakes in optical character recognition. Wrong or impossible spellings result in losing hits and/or returning wrong hits. A number of procedures have been implemented to increase the accuracy,

[13] https://bitbucket.org/timarkh/uniparser-grammar-eastern-armenian

[14] https://github.com/timarkh/tsakorpus

including human-assisted proofreading of the most important texts.

As mentioned above, most of the press corpus has been downloaded from the open electronic archives, which means that these periodicals are extremely over represented in EANC.

An important problem is the absence of syntactic and morphosyntactic markup. MEA is rich in periphrastic constructions in verbal morphology which are ignored by the parser. One of the perspectives of the project could be the implementation of basic collocation markup, including markup of auxiliary verb constructions. Now, querying these constructions is only possible indirectly (such as submitting context queries for converbs plus the verb *'to be'*, although these queries are obviously not enough restrictive).

Ignoring the context also leads to significant number of ambiguous cases in parsing results, which, for some queries, is a strong 'noise' factor. One of the solutions is human-assisted ambiguity removal.

In some cases, the two (or more) grammatical analyses of a wordform are by far not equally probable. It is possible to decrease the probability rank for less probable analyses depending on the context. Applying statistical procedures may be used to decrease the rank of morphosyntactic interpretations that are impossible or improbable in some types of contexts. For selected highly frequent cases of an extremely improbable homonymy, second readings have already been eliminated (e.g. the locative *asum* from the noun *as*).

Another useful development prospective would be allowing for context output provided with morphological glossing, more convenient for users coming from the field of linguistic typology and ready-to-use in typological publications which is already integrated in the updated version.

Providing the wordlist with phonetic tags indicating orthographically unpredictable phenomenon such as devoicing vs. non-devoicing after sonorants or between vowels or shwa insertion, orthographically would be a useful addon. Ultimately, that will provide a tool to show phonetic transcription of the word and wordform.

More detailed oral discourse transcription which requires serious theoretic background would also be a precious extension for the oral sub-corpus. Discourse transcription segments discourse into units with time synchronization for each unit; designates pauses, both silent (i.e. complete absence of verbal expression) and filled pauses (cf. English *'um', 'uh'* etc.); and tracks other phenomena peculiar to oral discourse, e.g. parceling, embeddings, discourse markers, etc. The transcripts should also be synchronized with light versions of audio files so that the user may not only read the transcript but also listen to the original audio.

An attempt of dialect corpus was made in the framework of EANC research grant project during 2008-2009. Interviews and narratives in three dialects of Armenian (1. Arcvaberd dialect (Shamshadin, Tavush region), 2. Shenavan dialect (Aparan, Aragatsotn region), 3. Gusana dialect (Maralik, Shirak region)) were collected and transcribed by three postgraduate grantee students in Yerevan. The target size of each corpus is 15 hours of recordings or about 100,000 tokens. The data is lemmatized and is available for online search similar to EANC[15].

One of the most important developments of Armenian corpus processing is to have a multivariational with all the diachronical stages of the Armenian language on the one hand (Classical Armenian, Middle Armenian, Modern Armenian), and the language varieties of Modern Armenian continuum (Modern Western Armenian, Armenian dialects, oral standards).

To address the existing drawbacks and outlined perspectives mentioned above, the project Digitizing Armenian Linguistic Heritage: Armenian Multivariational Corpus and Data Processing (DALiH)[16] was designed. The project aims at building for the first time an open-access and open-source unified digital linguistic platform for the whole spectrum of Armenian language variation. Each language variety will be represented by a comprehensive corpus which will be provided with full morphological annotation. More particularly, DALiH will be the first to design six new annotated corpora for 1) Classical Armenian; 2) Modern Western Armenian; 3) a pilot corpus of Middle Armenian; 4) three pilot corpora of dialects, and 5) one updated Modern Eastern Armenian corpus on the basis of EANC.

More particularly, the following updates will be proposed for MEA:

a. EANC database will be completed by compilation of new texts (10M tokens of various genres, about 50M tokens coming from Wikipedia and Wikisource, about 200M tokens from general Google database);

b. EANC rule-based annotation model will be accompanied by RNN, transformer-based and hybrid models in order to attune the ambiguity and to provide context-based (hence future syntactic) annotation;

c. EANC grammatical dictionary will be updated with new lexemes compiled from the most frequent unrecognized tokens of the corpus;

d. golden standard annotated written and oral corpora will be provided;

e. EANC oral sub-corpus will be sound-aligned;

f. ASR model will be elaborated on the basis of the aligned oral corpus.

DALiH started in April 2021 and the project will be launched in 2025.

8. Bibliographical References:

Ağayan, E. (1976). Արդի հայերենի բացատրական բառարան (Explanatory dictionary of Modern Armenian language). V. 1-2. Yerevan.

Avetisyan, K. and Ghukasyan, T. (2019). Word Embeddings for the Armenian Language: Intrinsic and Extrinsic Evaluation. arXiv:1906.03134 [cs].

Donabedian-Demopoulos, A. and Boyacioglu, N. (2007). La lemmatisation de l'arménien occidental

[15] http://web-corpora.net/EANC_dialects/search/

[16] http://www.inalco.fr/actualite/projet-prc-dalih-digitizing-armenian-linguistic-heritage-laureat-aapg-2021-anr.

The project DALiH is funded by French National Research Agency ANR-21-CE38-0006.

avec NooJ. S. Koeva, D. Maurel, M. Silberztein. *Formaliser les langues avec l'ordinateur, de INTEX à NooJ*, Presses Universitaires de Franche Comté, pp. 55-75.

Galstyan, E. (1985). Հայ-ռուսերեն բառարան (Armenian-Russian Dictionary). Yerevan.

Ghukasyan, T., Davtyan, G., Avetisyan, K. and Andrianov, I. (2018). pioNER: Datasets and baselines for Armenian named entity recognition. In *Proceedings of Ivannikov Ispras Open Conference (ISPRAS)*, pp. 56–61. IEEE.

Grgearian, A. and Harutyunian, N. (1987-1989). Աշխարհագրական անունների բառարան (Dictionary of geographic names). Yerevan.

Gyurdjinian, D. (2005). Անուն խոսքի մասերի թվի կարգը արդի հայերենում. Քերականական բառարան-տեղեկատու (The category of number of nominals in Modern Armenian). Yerevan.

Gyurdjinian, D. and Hekekian, N. (2007). Հայերենում գործածվող տառային հապավումների բառարան (Dictionary of acronyms used in Armenian). Yerevan.

Malajyan, A., Avetisyan, K., Ghukasyan, T. (2020). ARPA: Armenian Paraphrase Detection Corpus and Models. In *Proceedings of Ivannikov Memorial Workshop (IVMEM)*, pp. 35-39.

McEnery, T. and Hardie, A. (2012). Corpus linguistics: method, theory and practice. Cambridge & New York, Cambridge University Press.

McEnery, T. and Wilson, A. (2001). Corpus linguistics: an introduction. Edinburgh, Edinburgh University Press.

Stefanowitsch, A. (2020). Corpus linguistics: A guide to the methodology (Textbooks in Language Sciences 7). Berlin: Language Science Press.

Vidal-Gorène, C., Khurshudyan, V. and Donabédian-Demopoulos, A. (2020). Recycling and Comparing Morphological Annotation Models for Armenian Diachronic-Variational Corpus Processing. *Proceedings of the 7th Workshop on NLP for Similar Languages, Varieties and Dialects*, 90-101.

Yavrumyan, M. and Danielyan A. (2020). Համընդհանուր կախվածություններ և հայերենի ծառադարանը (Universal Dependencies and Armenian Tree-Bank). *Lraber hasarakakan gitut'yunneri*, 231-244.

Yavrumyan, M. (2019). Տեքստի մեքենական հատույթավորումը արևելահայերենի շարահյուսական ծառերի UD_ARMENIAN-ArmTDP բանկում (Tokenization and Word Segmentation in the UD_ARMENIAN-ArmTDP treebank). *Banber Yerevani hamalsarani. Philology*, 2019 № 3 (30). Yerevan. Pp. 52-65.

Annexe 1: EANC grammatical tags

#	EANC Tag	Description	Traditional Armenian Label	Example
		Parts of Speech	**Խոսքի մասեր**	
1	N	Noun	Գոյական	*սեղան*
2	A	Adjective	Ածական	*գեղեցիկ*
3	V	Verb	Բայ	*կարդալ*
4	ADV	Adverb	Մակբայ	*արագ*
5	NUM	Numeral	Թվական	*երեք*
6	PRON	Pronoun	Դերանուն	*ես*
7	PREP	Preposition	Կապ	*առանց*
8	POST	Postposition	Կապ	*մեջ*
9	CONJ	Conjunction	Շաղկապ	*և*
10	PART	Particle	Եղանակավորող բառեր	*թերևս*
11	INTJ	Interjection	Ձայնարկություն	*վա՜յ*
		Parts of Speech: lexical subcategories		
12	S	Independent pronouns	Անկախ դերանուն	*նա*
13	Dem	Demonstrative pronoun	Ցուցական դերանուն	*այդ*
14	Intrg	Interrogative pronoun	Հարցական դերանուն	*ինչ*
15	Hum	Human noun or pronoun	Անձի առում	*մարդ*
16	Anim	Animate noun or pronoun	Շնչավոր	*գայլ*
17	Inanim	Inanimate noun or pronoun	Անշունչ	*սեղան*
18	Coll	Collective noun	Հավաքական գոյական	*խումբ*
19	Topn	Toponym	Տեղանուն	*Հայաստան*
20	Persn	First name	Անձնանուն	*Արմեն*
21	Famn	Family name	Ազգանուն	*Պետրոսյան*
22	Abbr	Abbreviation	Հապավում	*ԱՊՀ*
23	Card	Cardinal numeral	Քանակական թվական	*երեք*
24	Tr	Transitive verb	Անցողական բայ	*տալ*
25	Intr	Intransitive verb	Անանցողական բայ	*վազել*
		Nominalization		
26	Inf	Infinitive	Անորոշ դերբայ	*կարդալ*
27	Rel	Relational noun	-	*սեղանինը*
28	Nmlz	Nominalized attribute (adjective, participle, genitive)	Գոյականացված (ածական, դերբայ, սեռական)	*գեղեցիկը, կարդացածը, սեղանինը*
		Case	**Հոլով**	
29	Nom	Nominative	Ուղղական	*քաղաք*
30	Gen	Genitive	Սեռական	*քաղաքի*
31	Dat	Dative	Տրական	*քաղաքին*
32	Abl	Ablative	Բացառական	*քաղաքից*
33	Ins	Instrumental	Գործիական	*քաղաքով*
34	Loc	Locative	Ներգոյական	*քաղաքում*

#	EANC Tag	Description	Traditional Armenian Label	Example
		Number	**Թիվ**	
35	Sg	Singular (nouns, pronouns or verbs)	Եզակի	*քաղաք*
36	Pl	Plural (nouns, pronouns or verbs)	Հոգնակի	*քաղաքներ*
37	Apl	Associative plural (nouns and pronouns)	հավաքական անեզական հոգնակի	*Վարդանանց*
		Determination/Possession	**Առում**	
38	Def	Definite form of a noun	Որոշյալ	*քաղաքը*
39	Poss1	First person possessed noun	Ստացական հոդ 1	*քաղաքս*
40	Poss2	Second person possessed noun	Ստացական հոդ 2	*քաղաքդ*
		Degree of Comparison	**Համեմատական աստիճան**	
41	Sup	Superlative	Գերադրական աստիճան	*ամենագեղեցիկ*
		Converb		
42	Cvb	Converb	Դերբայ	
43	Sim	Simultaneous converb	Անկատար դերբայ II	*կարդալիս*
44	Ipfv	Imperfective converb	Անկատար դերբայ I	*կարդում*
45	Pfv	Perfective converb	Վաղակատար դերբայ	*կարդացել*
46	Des	Destinative (future converb)	Ապառնի I	*կարդալու*
47	Conneg	Connegative converb	Ժխտական դերբայ	*կարդա*
		Participle		
48	Ptcp	Participle	Դերբայ	
49	Sbj	Subject participle	Ենթակայական դերբայ	*կարդացող*
50	Res	Resultative participle	Հարակատար դերբայ	*կարդացած*
		Valency Changing		
51	Caus	Causative (morphological)	Պատճառական	*վախեցնել*
52	Med	Medial (passive)	Կրավորական	*կառուցվել*
		Tense-Aspect-Mood	**Ժամանակ-Կերպ-Եղանակ**	
53	Pres	Present	Ներկա	*է*
54	Past	Past	Անցյալ	*էր*
55	Aor	Aorist	Անցյալ կատարյալ	*կարդաց*
56	Sbjv	Subjunctive	Ըղձական	*կարդա*
57	Cond	Conditional	Պայմանական	*կկարդա*
58	Imp	Imperative	Հրամայական	*կարդա՛*
		Polarity		
59	Neg	Negative form of a verb	Ժխտական	*չկարդաց*
		Person		
60	1	1st person category	Առաջին դեմք	*եմ*
61	2	2nd person category	Երկրորդ դեմք	*ես*
62	3	3rd person category	Երրորդ դեմք	*է*

Proceedings of the Workshop on Processing Language Variation: Digital Armenian (DigitAm 2022) @LREC2022, pages 38–42
Marseille, 20 June 2022

Towards a Unified ASR System for the Armenian Standards

Samuel Chakmakjian[1,2], Ilaine Wang[2]
[1]SeDyL (CNRS-Inalco), [2]ERTIM (Inalco)
7 rue Guy Môquet 94800 Villejuif, 2 rue de Lille 75007 Paris
{samuel.chakmakjian, ilaine.wang}@inalco.fr

Abstract

Armenian is a traditionally under-resourced language, which has seen a recent uptick in interest in the development of its tools and presence in the digital domain. Some of this recent interest has centred around the development of Automatic Speech Recognition (ASR) technologies. However, the language boasts two standard variants which diverge on multiple typological and structural levels. In this work, we examine some of the available bodies of data for ASR construction, present the challenges in the processing of these data and propose a methodology going forward.

Keywords: speech corpus, ASR, forced alignment

1. The Problem

Armenian is a traditionally under-resourced language, which has seen a recent uptick in interest in the development of its tools and presence in the digital domain. Some of this recent interest has centred around the development of Automatic Speech Recognition (ASR) technologies. However, the language boasts two standard variants which diverge on multiple typological and structural levels.

1.1. A Tale of Two Phonologies

This structural divide is the most salient at a phonetic-phonological level, with Standard Eastern Armenian's (SEA) phonemic inventory containing 36 phonemes (30 consonants, 6 vowels), and Standard Western Armenian's (SWA) inventory being comprised of 30 phonemes (24 consonants, 6 vowels).

The vocalic systems of SEA and SWA are largely the similar, with the five cardinal vowels /i, e, a, o, u/ and a mid-central vowel /ə/. The consonant systems share the same nasals, fricatives, and approximants (/m, n, f, v, s, z, ʃ, ʒ, χ, ʁ, h, j, l/). SEA distinguishes between two rhotics, a tap /ɾ/ and a trill /r/, whereas SWA does not make such a distinction. The most problematic feature of the divergence in phonologies however, is that of the plosive and affricate series in SWA and SEA. SEA's plosive and affricate phonemes have a three-way voicing distinction: voiced, voiceless, and voiceless aspirated. Modern SWA has a two-way voicing system of voiced and voiceless aspirated. The plosive and affricates phonemes of SEA are therefore the following: /b, p, p^h, d, t, t^h, g, k, k^h, dz, ts, ts^h, dʒ, tʃ, $tʃ^h$/, and the plosive and affricate phonemes of SWA are as follows: /b, p^h, d, t^h, g, k^h, dz, ts^h, dʒ, $tʃ^h$/.

Table 1 provides an example of the diverging phonetic realisations of three similar items.

Item	SEA	SWA	Translation
⟨ բառ ⟩	[**b**ɑɾ]	[**p^h**ɑɾ]	'word'
⟨ պար ⟩	[**p**ɑɾ]	[**b**ɑɾ]	'dance'
⟨ փառ ⟩	[**p^h**ɑɾ]	[**p^h**ɑɾ]	'placenta'

Table 1: Three words and their pronunciations in SEA *vs.* SWA

1.2. Towards a Multivariant Culture

Despite this divergence in phonemic inventories, many factors render a unified system preferable. The two variants share a writing system and base lexicon, and while the two variants may be clearly distinct from one another, their speech communities are not. Amongst proficient speakers, there is a high level of mutual intelligibility. Furthermore, the social realities of increased contact between speakers of SEA (traditionally found in the Republic of Armenia, Iran and countries of the post-Soviet zone) and speakers of SWA (traditionally found in post-Ottoman diasporan communities founded in the Middle East, Europe and the Americas) manifest in multivariant households, and sometimes multivariant speakers.

An increasing presence of SEA speakers in traditionally SWA-speaking diasporan communities, and an increasing presence of SWA in the Republic of Armenia (a traditionally SEA-speaking zone) pose more of a technical problem than a social one. While speakers frequently overcome these barriers, it would be very challenging for a single-variant ASR system to generate automatic subtitles for a video of a SEA-speaking journalist and a SWA-speaking interviewee, or a discussion between a SWA-speaking educator and a SEA-speaking student. If single-variant ASR were employed for the purposes of home-assistant technologies, a device would risk understanding one spouse in a multivariant household, and not the other.

Armenian's orthography (in both variants) is largely phonemic (Vaux, 1998), and maintains a representation of three graphemes for each of the plosive/affricate voicing sequences, making rule-based speech synthesis of either pronunciation feasible from the same text. However, producing text from speech input poses a challenge when some acoustically identical inputs correspond to the same grapheme, while other sets of identical input are to be recognised as different graphemes.

Armenian can be described as a pluricentric language (Cowe, 1992; Muhr, 2016). We can draw inspiration from attempts that have been made to construct ASR systems for other pluricentric languages. Many attempts rely at their core on a Grapheme to Phoneme approach (G2P) (Bisani and Ney, 2008). For example for Spanish, Caballero et al. (2009) define a "...multidialectal phone set [which] leads to a full dialect-independent recognizer." Another approach builds off of the process of discriminating between similar languages (DSL) (Zampieri et al., 2017) in creating a mechanism to determine which variant of a multivariant language is being spoken, such as the case of Arabic (Ali, 2018). Attempts at solving this issue for Armenian will rely upon a combination of these two approaches, due to the complication of Armenian's phone sets including an inversion and a merger.

Recent literature acknowledges a slight performance gap, with end-to-end (E2E) ASR systems slightly under-performing when compared to hybrid ASR models[1], but also, that recent innovations are closing that gap (Perero-Codosero et al., 2022). We will present our preliminary study of the main phonemic considerations which are a challenge for an ASR system to address the SEA:SWA variation issue. Our work to construct an ASR model for Armenian is conducted in the framework of the DALiH project, within which we expect to take advantage of the two major transcribed audio corpora, described in Section 3. Those will be used to implement E2E and hybrid models which, in turn, will be used in comparative/contrastive studies to have a more informed view of how SEA:SWA variations can be efficiently taken into account by a unified ASR system.

2. The State of Armenian ASR

The budding presence of ASR technologies for Armenian is underway, however there often exist many roadblocks in terms of access of information, material and data for the scientific and research communities. We can group the attempts to approach Armenian ASR into two categories: (1) multilingual approaches which include Armenian, and (2) Armenian-specific approaches.

[1]Especially in langauges other than English.

2.1. Multilingual Models

In the case of (1) one can site companies who create models adapted to multiple languages. For example, Happy Scribe[2], a company based in Barcelona, Spain, proposes an automatic transcription and automatic subtitling service for 63 languages, including Armenian. Another such example is VocalMatic[3], based in Toronto, Canada. Similarly to Happy Scribe, VocalMatic boasts speech-to-text models for more than 100 languages (including Armenian). Lastly, amongst the three corporations often credited with bringing ASR technology into private homes via personal assistants (Google, Amazon, and Apple), only Google has a voice recognition option for Armenian at present[4]. In none of the aforementioned instances is the variant of Armenian specified, but when this is the case, the underlying assumption is that "Armenian" refers only to SEA. Otherwise, the variant or dialect would be specified[5].

2.2. Armenian-specific Models

In regards to case (2), Armenian-specific approaches date back at least to 2016, such as the system of Vardanyan (2016), an ASR system constructed based on tools from the open-source CMUSphynx project[6]. Another important Armenian-specific project is that of the National Center of Communication and Artificial Intelligence Technologies (NCCAIT[7]), which builds its corpus progressively through audio submissions provided by volunteers who read pre-selected texts. These two projects work on SEA primarily, but recently, the NCCAIT introduced a new analogous, but seemingly separate project[8] which operates in a similar manner for SWA.

Both the multilingual approaches and Armenian-specific approaches are promising in that they show evidence of the advancement of the technology, however the multilingual approaches are all explicitly private, and it remains unclear whether the NCCAIT resources will ultimately be open-source. The broader scientific community therefore lacks access to their information,

[2]https://www.happyscribe.com/transcribe-armenian

[3]https://vocalmatic.com/languages/transcribe-armenian-armenian-to-text

[4]Google Translation has speech-to-text capacities for Armenian, indicated by the microphone button in the input box https://translate.google.com/?hl=fr&sl=hy&tl=en&op=translate

[5]For example, Vardanyan (2016) wrote an entire master's thesis on the creation of an "Armenian" ASR system, in which the variant is never specified, all of the data and analyses pertain exclusively to SEA

[6]https://cmusphinx.github.io

[7]http://3.144.127.191/mt/#

[8]https://aws.ican24.net/hywrec/index.php

training corpora, and above all, the methodologies behind the creation of their systems. Furthermore, none of the programmes mentioned above have the explicit objective of functioning on a bi-variant basis; they either ignore this complication (by referring only to "Armenian", understood to mean SEA) or in the case of NCCAIT, they isolate the variants from each other in constructing separate models.

3. Resources

While Armenian has traditionally been considered an under-resourced language when compared to languages of wider-spread speakerships, the language benefits from a developed literary history and extensive textual corpora. In recent years, significant advances have been made in the digitisation of Armenian texts, and the compilation of oral corpora as well. Any further research into the development and refining of Armenian ASR technologies will depend on bare audio data for processing, as well as transcribed and aligned audio data for verification and training. Our research within the DALiH framework will benefit from two major available oral corpora, one of each of the standard variants.

3.1. Available Speech Corpora

3.1.1. Western Armenian

A major source of audio data for standard Western Armenian is the Rerooted[9] archive, an archive of interviews carried out starting in 2017 with Western Armenian speakers from Syria, who relocated to the Republic of Armenia as a result of the war in their birth country. Each interview generally last between 45 minutes and 1.5 hours, in which an interviewer poses question (often in Western Armenian, but sometimes in English) and the interviewee responds at length in Western Armenian. The vast majority of the audio documents available are not only transcribed in SWA, but also translated into English, as the project's primary goal concerns the transmission of memory of a displaced community. The full length interviews are available through the Rerooted website and housed on YouTube, where the transcriptions and translations serve as subtitles (and are therefore aligned by phrase). These aligned transcriptions were produced using the online subtitling platform Amara[10], from where we have been granted access to the aligned transcriptions in SRT (standard subtitling) format. In the framework of the DALiH project, we aim to make these resources publicly available as well. In total the exploitable aligned audio data from the Rerooted archive amounts to 90 documents, or 81 hours and forty minutes.

3.1.2. Eastern Armenian

A primordial source of Eastern Armenian audio data is the Eastern Armenian National Corpus (Khurshudian

[9] https://www.rerooted.org

[10] https://amara.org/fr/

	Interviews	Hours
Translated (ENG)	100	87:46:03
Transcribed (ARM) + aligned	90	81:39:41
Total available	102	89:50:04

Table 2: Rerooted Archives' database

and Daniel, 2009)[11] (EANC), an online written and speech corpus compiled by an international team of linguists, scholars and software professionals, in the framework of an eponymous project launched in 2006. Amongst EANC's collected and processed materials are audio data of diverse genres: spontaneous speech, public discourse, online communications and task-oriented discourse. All together the aforementioned materials amount to 774 transcribed audio documents, or 3.5 million tokens.[12]

Rerooted and EANC both provide a healthy base of semi-processed audio data, originating from speakers of diverse ages and backgrounds, upon which further research and testing of ASR models will depend.

3.2. Data Preprocessing

None of the two corpora described in this section were built to train an ASR model. The use of such resources therefore requires preprocessing.
As mentioned in the previous section, most of Rerooted videos already have subtitles in Armenian. No further data processing is needed other than a trivial format conversion, from SRT to TextGrid[13]. Such conversion is useful as we are using Praat (Boersma and Weenink, 2022) to visualise the data and running Praat scripts to study variant-related phenomena.

On the other hand, transcriptions for EANC have to be aligned to be used. Considering the amount of data to be processed, we developed a simple automatic processing chain:

1. Extraction of the transcription from Word files
2. Automatic segmentation into utterances, units that are broadly equivalent to sentences in written texts
3. Forced alignment of those units with the sound

Extraction of the transcription While subtitles only transcribe what was pronounced by speakers, transcriptions meant to be analysed by linguists also contain extralinguistic information such as the speaker's attitude,

[11] http://www.eanc.net

[12] Unfortunately we cannot report the quantity of data in hours, because that information is unavailable to us.

[13] The conversion was successfully tested on a sample using a slightly modified version of the script available on https://github.com/tanmaysurana/srt2textgrid.

laughs, pauses or overlapping sequences, as shown in Figure 1. In this example, we can see that the annotator explicitly indicated that the two speakers were "talking at the same time", using a specific marker, #, to signal that this is not a transcription but an annotation. The first step of our processing chain consists of removing this extralinguistic information along with the speaker's identification which can be either their name, their status (Բժիշկ *doctor*, Աշխատող *employee* etc.) or an identification code (S1/S2, Կ1/Կ2 etc.).

Կ2@ .. է հա / ասա բռնի / .. ի՞նչ օգուտ։ // ..
Ամեն տարի ծաղկում է՛ / .. ու տենց ցուրտը
տանում / ու մնում ենք առանց միրգ։ #ԽՈՍՈՒՄ
ԵՆ ՄԻԱԺԱՄԱՆԱԿ#
Կ1@ էս ծիրանները չփչանա։ // #ԽՈՍՈՒՄ ԵՆ
ՄԻԱԺԱՄԱՆԱԿ# .. Ծիրանի **ծառները** / .. շատ
սիրուն են / .. ոնց որ հարս լինի։

Figure 1: Excerpt of the transcription of a dialogue from EANC [dialogue_in_the_shop1]
translation:
K1@ Well yeah / I said hold / .. what's the use.// .. Every year it blossoms / .. and that kind of cold in the house / and we remain without fruit. #TALKING AT THE SAME TIME#
K2@ don't let these apricots spoil. // #TALKING AT THE SAME TIME# the apricot ***trees*** *are very pretty/ .. like a bride would be.*

Automatic segmentation Text segmentation is necessary for alignment. Speech data typically does not have punctuation and automatic speech segmentation may therefore rely on prosodic cues (such as lengthening of vowels or contours) or the length of pauses between words. However, EANC's transcription guidelines seem to include punctuation marks as well as segmentation marks in some cases such as in Figure 1 where / and // seem to be used to segment the utterances into smaller units. The second step of our processing chain made use of punctuation marks (namely, the comma and the :[14] (*verjaket*) used as a full stop) and :// in dialogues[15].

Forced alignment Aligning orthographic transcriptions with their corresponding speech is a costly task in terms of time. For the last part of our processing chain, we use a well-documented Python package for forced alignment called aeneas (Pettarin, 2022)[16]. This decision was mainly led by the fact that it wraps eSpeak[17], an open-source speech synthesizer, allowing support for both standards of Armenian. Even if this support has been implemented naively with no feedback neither from Eastern nor Western Armenian native speakers yet, preliminary results are quite good for high quality recordings.

The alignment was manually evaluated by a native speaker on a small sample of different types of speech from EANC:

- monologues including TV speech recordings and interviews in which the interviewer only asks a question at the very beginning of the recordings;
- dialogues : conversations with two participants (on the phone, at the office, when shopping etc.).
- polylogues : conversations with more than two participants, such as friends having a meal together.

It is noteworthy that there is a discrepancy in the quality of those samples, some being recorded in a quiet room, while others were recorded in the street where cars or construction work can be heard in the background. Unsurprisingly, the results are unequal: very good on monologues (especially for the interviews) but quite bad on polylogues, especially with noise in the background and/or when speakers' speech overlaps frequently. While the use of our aligner is promising on monologues, we now have to do a formal evaluation to assess whether or not providing our annotators with automatically aligned recordings of polylogues will help them or if segmenting from scratch takes less time than the manual correction of segments' boundaries.

4. A Unified System

As explained in Section 2, while advances in Armenian ASR are well underway, there remain large issues in terms of availability to the academic community. Additionally, none of the existing projects propose a model which addresses the community's need for a unified, or bi-variant system. In order to proceed forward in this research, and keeping in mind the limitations of resources, we propose that a hybrid method is more appropriate in the immediate future than an End-to-end (E2E) ASR system. In following other recent approaches to automatic transcription for lesser-endowed languages (such as (Guillaume et al., 2022)), we suggest that a hybrid system would enable us to employ neuronal systems such as wav2vec for feature extraction, informing our acoustic model, which we would fine-tune manually. We would then pass to a sole traditional lexicon model, and finally to a language model.

In employing this strategy, the pre-processing (i.e. alignment) and processing of audio data becomes all the more crucial in order to train our model, and also to measure it's efficacy and accuracy.

[14]The *verjaket* looks like a Latin colon but is part of the Armenian script and is encoded U+0589 in Unicode, so this punctuation mark is quite reliable as a segmenter.

[15]We decided not to use / as a segmentation mark because such units would be too small.

[16]Freely available on https://github.com/readbeyond/aeneas/.

[17]http://espeak.sourceforge.net/

5. Conclusion

We have outlined the major challenges in the development of Armenian ASR, especially as it pertains to a system which would understand both of the language's standard variants. Despite major advancements in Armenian ASR, this central issue remains largely unaddressed. We present the available oral corpora, and with the data available to us we ran a preliminary forced-alignment test, which showed varying results, confirming the need for the development of tools and resources. Lastly we proposed a basic methodology for moving forward.

6. Acknowledgements

DALiH (*Digitizing Armenian Linguistic Heritage*) is a project funded by the ANR, the French National Research Agency (ANR-21-CE38-0006).

7. Bibliographical References

Ali, A. M. A. M. (2018). *Multi-dialect Arabic broadcast speech recognition*. Ph.D. thesis.

Bisani, M. and Ney, H. (2008). Joint-sequence models for grapheme-to-phoneme conversion. *Speech communication*, 50(5):434–451.

Boersma, P. and Weenink, D. (2022). Praat: doing phonetics by computer [Computer program]. Version 6.2.12, retrieved 26 April 2022 from http://www.praat.org/.

Caballero, M., Moreno, A., and Nogueiras, A. (2009). Multidialectal spanish acoustic modeling for speech recognition. *Speech Communication*, 51(3):217–229.

Cowe, P. (1992). Amn tel hay kay: Armenian as a pluricentric language. *M. Clyne*.

Guillaume, S., Wisniewski, G., Galliot, B., Nguyễn, M.-C., Fily, M., Jacques, G., and Michaud, A. (2022). Plugging a neural phoneme recognizer into a simple language model: a workflow for low-resource settings. working paper or preprint, March.

Khurshudian, V. and Daniel, M. (2009). Eastern Armenian National Corpus. In *Computational Linguistics and Intellectual Technologies: Papers from the Annual International Conference "Dialogue'2009"*, pages 509–518.

Muhr, R. (2016). The state of the art of research on pluricentric languages: Where we were and where we are now. *Pluricentric Languages and Non-Dominant Varieties Worldwide, Österreichisches deutsch sprache der gegenwart*, 18:13–40.

Perero-Codosero, J. M., Espinoza-Cuadros, F. M., and Hernández-Gómez, L. A. (2022). A comparison of hybrid and end-to-end asr systems for the iberspeech-rtve 2020 speech-to-text transcription challenge. *Applied Sciences*, 12(2):903.

Pettarin, A. (2022). aeneas [Computer program]. Version 1.7.3, retrieved 26 April 2022 from https://www.readbeyond.it/aeneas/.

Vardanyan, A. (2016). Noise-robust speech recognition system for armenian language. Master's thesis, American University of Armenia.

Vaux, B. (1998). *The phonology of Armenian*. Oxford University Press.

Zampieri, M., Malmasi, S., Ljubešić, N., Nakov, P., Ali, A., Tiedemann, J., Scherrer, Y., and Aepli, N. (2017). Findings of the vardial evaluation campaign 2017. In *Proceedings of the fourth workshop on NLP for similar languages, varieties and dialects*.

Author Index